PROBLE
MANAGE

BCS, THE CHARTERED INSTITUTE FOR IT

BCS, The Chartered Institute for IT champions the global IT profession and the interests of individuals engaged in that profession for the benefit of all. We promote wider social and economic progress through the advancement of information technology, science and practice. We bring together industry, academics, practitioners and government to share knowledge, promote new thinking, inform the design of new curricula, shape public policy and inform the public.

Our vision is to be a world-class organisation for IT. Our 70,000 strong membership includes practitioners, businesses, academics and students in the UK and internationally. We deliver a range of professional development tools for practitioners and employees. A leading IT qualification body, we offer a range of widely recognised qualifications.

Further Information
BCS, The Chartered Institute for IT,
First Floor, Block D,
North Star House, North Star Avenue,
Swindon, SN2 1FA, United Kingdom.
T +44 (0) 1793 417 424
F +44 (0) 1793 417 444
www.bcs.org/contact

http://shop.bcs.org/

PROBLEM MANAGER
Careers in IT service management

Colin Rudd

Published by BCS Learning & Development Ltd, a wholly owned subsidiary of BCS, The Chartered Institute for IT, First Floor, Block D, North Star House, North Star Avenue, Swindon, SN2 1FA, UK. www.bcs.org

ISBN: 978-1-78017-237-8

This edition is for sale in Indian subcontinent only. Not for export elsewhere.

British Cataloguing in Publication Data.
A CIP catalogue record for this book is available at the British Library.

BCS books are available at special quantity discounts to use as premiums and sale promotions, or for use in corporate training programmes. Please visit our Contact Us page at www.bcs.org/contact

Typeset by Lapiz Digital Services, Chennai, India.
Printed and bound in India by Saurabh Printers, New Delhi.

CONTENTS

LIST OF FIGURES AND TABLES

AUTHOR

Colin Rudd has worked in the IT industry for over 40 years. He has in excess of 20 years' practical experience of service management and is internationally recognised as a leading authority, coach, mentor, trainer and practitioner on all aspects of service management. He has been heavily involved in the development of ITIL® as an architect and lead author, having been involved in every version of ITIL to date. Colin was also involved in the development of the Skills Framework for the Information Age (SFIA) and its predecessor the Industry Structure Model (ISM). Colin now works for his own company using his extensive service management experience and knowledge to assist many client organisations with the improvement of their processes and solutions.

He has delivered many organisational benefits through the implementation of successful problem management activities and has been a successful problem manager for several organisations. He has extensive practical experience of the use and application of problem management methods, techniques and processes.

He has delivered service management consultancy and training all over the world including keynote presentations at many national and international conferences. Colin also assisted with the development of the ISO/IEC 20000 service management standard and the ISO/IEC 20000 certification and qualification schemes. He was recently the chairman of *it*SMF UK and a director of *it*SMF international. His enormous contributions to the service management industry were recognised in 2002 with the presentation of the *it*SMF's lifetime achievement award.

FOREWORD

I recall early in my service management experience carrying a pager and knowing that if it went off I was required in the situation room. Whether it involved the data centre, an application or even that we had missed a critical deadline, the mandate was 'all hands on deck' to solve the 'problem'. A problem manager would be identified and we would ship in pizza, water and camp beds because no one was leaving until the situation was resolved.

Today the pagers are replaced by mobile phones and the situation room is replaced by web conferencing, but for many, problem management remains a critical reactive activity.

But effective problem management is so much more that this. Having been involved in service management for most of my career from banking, to software, to the development of industry standards, I have been a strong advocate of the notion that problem management done well is one of the most pivotal roles in service management.

In this disruptive, hybrid cloud world where every service delivered in the business is dependent on technology for its very existence, effective problem management simply must be proactive. Mature organisations will have problem managers that focus on potential issues and problems and engaging stakeholders in advance of their occurrence, taking action to reduce the risk and impact of potential problems to drive outcomes that should result in less critical outages.

In short, the role of the problem manager is critical to the success of today's modern business, yet many organisations have not given the role the attention, focus and resourcing required to deliver organisational value. One might argue that this is due to the lack of definitive guidance in the space – guidance that marries good practices, career path and process together.

I have known Colin Rudd as an author, practitioner and educator for many years and spent countless hours debating the problem manager role, its lack of adoption and often-ineffective results. In this book, Colin masterfully draws together different roles that the problem manager can take depending on the organisation, linking the role to key activities and most importantly, identifying the skills and capabilities required. This is not a theoretical publication; its power is in the practicality of the guidance, allowing the problem management role to become one of the most pivotal roles in the delivery of IT-powered business.

As you read this book I challenge you to leverage the user stories, case studies and information on frameworks and apply them practically to your role. Use this book to challenge yourself to become a better problem manager and drive value in your organisation. The overarching theme has to be to mature your processes so that you can move to being proactive in your role, while adding value and testing the culture and organisation efficacy in dealing with problems. One thing I have learned in effective risk management is that you cannot mitigate all risk, so knowing and having practised what to do in a likely problem scenario is critical, and only with preparation will you be effective.

This book provides the guidance to ensure that problem management is not simply a service management role, it is pivotal to the success of your organisation and career.

Happy reading, and I wish you all the success in your career.

Robert E Stroud CGEIT CRISC
International President ISACA®
VP Strategy & Innovation CA Technologies
@RobertEStroud

ACKNOWLEDGEMENT

The author would like to acknowledge and thank Steve Rudd of Thomson Reuters for his significant contributions to the material contained within this publication.

ABBREVIATIONS

BCM	Business continuity management
BCS	BCS, The Chartered Institute for IT
BIA	Business impact analysis
CAB	Change advisory board
CFIA	Component failure impact analysis
CI	Configuration item
CIO	Chief IT officer
CMDB	Configuration management database
CMS	Configuration management system
COBIT®	Control Objectives for Information and related Technology
CPS	Creative problem solving
CRM	Customer relationship management
CSF	Critical success factor
CSI	Continual service improvement
DSS	Deliver, Service and Support within COBIT®
ISACA®	Previously known as the Information Systems Audit and Control Association, but ISACA® is now known by its acronym only
ISM	Industry Structure Model
IT	Information technology
IT4IT	An IT consortium
ITSCM	IT service continuity management
KEDB	Known error database

KPI	Key performance indicator
MPR	Major problem review
PDCA	Plan, Do, Check, Act, sometimes shown as P-D-C-A
PIR	Post-implementation reviews
RACI	Responsibility, accountability, consulted and informed, referring to a chart used to indicate the involvement of individuals within process activities
RCA	Root cause analysis
RFC	Request for change
SAC	Service acceptance criteria
SACM	Service asset and configuration management
SFA	Service failure analysis
SFIA	Skills Framework for the Information Age
SIP	Service improvement plan
SKMS	Service knowledge management system
SLA	Service level agreement
SLM	Service level management
SMS	Service management system
SPoF	Single point of failure
TOP	Technical observation post
VBF	Vital business function

GLOSSARY

Some of these definitions here and within the chapters are from ITIL publications. © Crown copyright material is reproduced with the permission of the controller of AXELOS.

Autonomation The use of automation with a human touch, involving the appropriate use of automation for the management of production systems and workflows.

Event A change in state that has significance for the management of a service or other configuration item.

Incident An unplanned interruption to an IT service or reduction in the quality of an IT service.

Incident management The process for managing the lifecycle of all incidents. Incident management ensures that normal service operation is restored as quickly as possible and the business impact is minimised.

Knowledge article An item or artefact of information or knowledge stored within a knowledge base or the service knowledge management system (SKMS).

Knowledge base A logical database containing data and information used by the service knowledge management system (SKMS).

Known error A problem that has a root cause and a workaround.

Known error database A database containing all known error records.

Problem   A cause of one or more incidents.

Problem management   The process for managing the lifecycle of all problems and known errors. Problem management proactively prevents incidents from happening and minimises the impact of incidents that cannot be prevented.

Risk   A possible event that could cause harm or loss, or affect the ability to achieve objectives.

Workaround   A means of reducing or eliminating the impact of an incident or problem for which a full resolution is not yet available.

1 INTRODUCTION

The purpose of this book is to describe the role of the problem manager and the activities and practices associated with the role. The role of the problem manager within an organisation varies considerably, based on the type and needs of the organisation involved.

This book examines and explains the different roles, activities, skills and capabilities required to perform effective problem management and the methods and techniques needed. It describes the role of a problem manager and explains the concepts, principles and techniques associated with problem management and their use within an organisation.

This book has also been written to provide advice and guidance, together with examples and case studies on the implementation and application of problem management activities and techniques within an organisation. Information is also included on industry frameworks and standards and on good industry practice within the area of problem management. The industry frameworks and standards principally referred to in this book are:

- **ITIL**: A set of best practice publications for IT service management. ITIL provides guidance on the processes, activities and functions required for the effective provision of quality IT services.[1]

---

[1] • ITIL (2011) Service Strategy. ISBN: 9780113313044.
- ITIL (2011) Service Design. ISBN: 9780113313051.
- ITIL (2011) Service Transition. ISBN: 9780113313068.
- ITIL (2011) Service Operation. ISBN: 9780113313075.
- ITIL (2011) Continual Service Improvement. ISBN: 9780113313082.

- **COBIT®**: Previously known as Control OBjectives for Information and related Technology (COBIT®) is a set of guidance for the management and governance of IT processes from the Information Systems Audit and Control Association (ISACA®).[2]

- **ISO/IEC 20000**: An international series of standards for IT service management from the International Organization for Standardization (ISO) that provide guidance on the requirements for an effective IT service management system.[3]

- **SFIA:** Skills Framework for the Information Age (SFIA),[4] from the SFIA Foundation, is a framework which defines the professional skills needed to perform activities across the full lifecycle of IT service provision. This publication contains information from SFIA with the permission of the SFIA Foundation.

---

[2] ISACA® (2012) COBIT 5 – Enabling Processes. ISACA®

[3] • ISO (2011) ISO/IEC 20000-1: Information technology – Service management – Part 1: Service management system requirements. International Organization for Standardization.
   • ISO (2012) ISO/IEC 20000-2: Information technology – Service management – Part 2: Guidance on the application of service management systems. International Organization for Standardization.

[4] SFIA (2011) SFIA 5 Framework reference. SFIA Foundation

2 OVERVIEW OF THE MANAGEMENT OF PROBLEMS

This book describes and explains the possible roles and activities of a problem manager, and this chapter provides an introduction to service management and specifically problem management.

INTRODUCTION TO SERVICE MANAGEMENT

The management of services and information is vital to the success of all organisations. The level of IT service delivered to the business has a major impact on the quality of the information and its accuracy, accessibility and availability. There are very few business processes that can run without the IT services that support them or the information those services provide. Many IT service provider organisations invest significant amounts of time and effort into the management and improvement of their IT services.

Problem management is a crucially important area of service management and improvement. The identification, analysis, reduction and resolution of problems and issues are key to the improvement of the quality and value of IT services. Problem management activities also provide essential information for many other areas, processes and functions.

INTRODUCTION TO PROBLEM MANAGEMENT

The area of problem management is extensive. This means that the role of a problem manager can also be extensive, covering all areas of issue resolution, including both incidents and problems. However, for the purposes of this book the role of the problem manager is principally confined to the management of problems and their associated activities.

A problem manager works to resolve issues and to minimise the adverse impact of these issues on the business of an organisation. Issues can be generally categorised within two broad areas: incidents and problems. These are defined as follows:

ITIL DEFINITIONS

Incident: An unplanned interruption to an IT service or reduction in the quality of an IT service.

Problem: A cause of one or more incidents.

ISO/IEC20000 DEFINITIONS

Incident: An unplanned interruption to a service, a reduction in the quality of a service or an event that has not yet impacted the service to the customer.

Problem: A root cause of one or more incidents.

ITIL DEFINITIONS

Incident management: The process for managing the lifecycle of all incidents. Incident management ensures that normal service operation is restored as quickly as possible and the business impact is minimised.

Problem management: The process for managing the lifecycle of all problems and known errors. Problem management proactively prevents incidents from happening and minimises the impact of incidents that cannot be prevented.

In contrast, the ISO/IEC 20000 standard defines the intent of the incident management and problem management processes as:

ISO/IEC 20000 DEFINITIONS

Incident management intent: The incident and service request process should manage incidents and service requests consistently to ensure that incident resolution or request fulfilment is achieved within agreed service targets and time frames.

Problem management intent: The problem management process identifies the unknown, underlying root causes of incidents and proposes permanent resolutions through the change management process. The problem management process also proactively prevents incidents from occurring through trend analysis and recommendations of preventative action.

The differences between the purpose and objectives of incident and problem management can lead to conflict between the two process areas.

EXAMPLE – INCIDENT AND PROBLEM MANAGEMENT

A server fails, causing slow response to the service that it supports. This event is detected by a management system, and the incident is recorded automatically on the service desk system.

This particular situation has happened many times in the past and there are a number of previous incident records (at least one for each occurrence of the event) linked to a problem record. The incidents have always been resolved in the past by reloading the server as soon as possible. Problem analysis of the previous incidents has been unable to determine the root cause of the incident due to the lack of diagnostic information from the server. So conflict now arises between incident and problem management:

- Incident management wants to reload the server as soon as possible again, to restore normal service to the users of the service.

- Problem management wants to keep the server in the current state and gather as much diagnostic information as possible so that they can determine the root cause of the problem and develop a resolution.

At some point a decision must to be made that the incidents are causing too much disruption and that problem management must be allowed time to gather the necessary information in order to analyse and resolve the underlying cause of the incidents. Otherwise the incidents will continue to occur.

This conflict between the two areas needs to be carefully managed and minimised.

So the role of a problem manager is to manage and resolve the cause of unplanned interruptions and issues (defects, failures or events), whether actual or potential, and to minimise the disruption they cause.

Incident management, on the other hand, is the process for managing the lifecycle of all incidents through the use of incident records. The focus of incident management is to restore normal service as soon as possible to affected areas, whereas problem management is the process for managing the lifecycle of all problems, through the use of problem records. The focus of problem management is the prevention of incidents and problems and the minimising of their adverse impact on the organisation by resolving the underlying root cause of incidents.

Therefore, there is considerable overlap and interaction between incident management activities and the activities involved in the management of problems. This means that the roles and activities described in this book will need to be adapted to meet the needs of the organisation and the activities and processes that exist within that organisation.

This book describes the potential activities within the role of a problem manager. It is for to the reader to adopt and adapt the contents of this book to fit their individual needs and the needs of their organisation in the management and resolution of incidents and problems.

Problem management and incident management are two of the principal process areas of one of the value chains/ streams identified by the IT4IT Consortium (a group of large organisations) in their IT4IT framework.[5] The four value streams identified are:

- **Strategy to portfolio value stream:** focusing on efficient IT investment to develop a comprehensive portfolio of services.

- **Requirement to deploy value stream:** taking business needs and demands, and deploying IT services and solutions to align with business requirements.

- **Request to fulfil value stream:** managing service requests instigated by the business, from initiation through to fulfilment.

- **Detect to correct value stream:** managing issues, events, defects or failures from detection through to resolution and correction.

---

[5] IT4IT (2013) Value Chain and Reference Architecture Overview, IT4IT Consortium

An overview of the main process areas within the 'detect to correct' value chain is illustrated in Figure 2.1.

Figure 2.1 The 'detect to correct' IT value chain

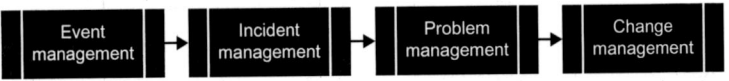

Issues are detected either automatically by systems and tools or by people reporting issues to the service desk. Incidents are managed through the service desk and the incident management process, whereas problems should be managed using the problem management process. These two process areas have different objectives and therefore different activities. This difference can be seen from the following:

> The role of a problem manager varies considerably from organisation to organisation and is dependent on the needs of the organisation. The range of problem manager roles extends from someone who manages or progresses incidents and problems from time to time to someone who manages and improves problem management and incident management methods and activities throughout an organisation.

Before problem management is described in detail, it is necessary to define a number of additional terms that are used within this book.

ITIL DEFINITIONS

Knowledge base: A logical database containing data and information used by the service knowledge management system (SKMS).

Known error: A problem that has a documented root cause and a workaround.

Workaround: A means of reducing or eliminating the impact of an incident or problem for which a full resolution is not yet available.

Knowledge article: An item or artefact of information or knowledge stored within a knowledge base or the service knowledge management system (SKMS).

ISO/IEC20000 DEFINITION

Known error: A problem that has an identified root cause or a method of reducing or eliminating its impact on a service by working around it.

This book assumes that roles and functions associated with incident management are already established, because these are prerequisites for the effective management of problems. The incident management process and database provide the basic input information on which a problem management process can start to be developed, and without it, it is almost impossible to start establishing problem management practices. The interactions between these two processes and the other main areas and processes are shown in Figure 2.2.

This interaction between incident and problem management, as well as the important interfaces and interactions between problem management and other areas and processes, are covered in more detail in 'Interfaces and dependencies' on page 40.

In practice, problem management is one of the processes that is poorly implemented within many organisations. The main reasons for this are that in many organisations, there is confusion over the difference between an incident and a problem, and about the requirements for their management.

Figure 2.2 The interaction between the key processes

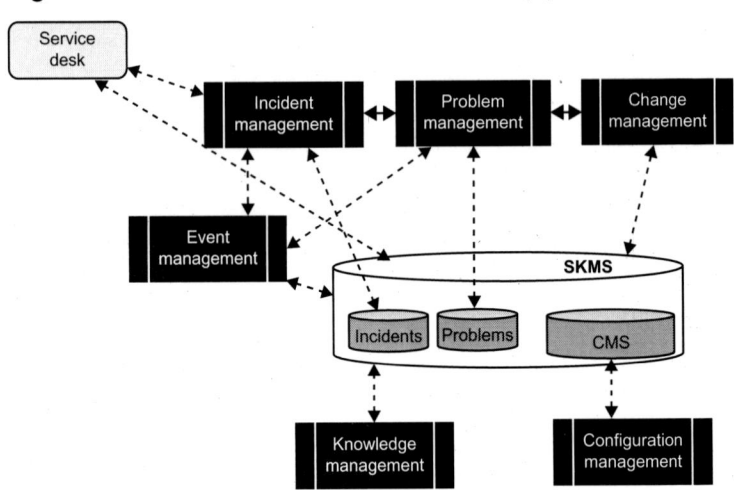

The following example of an everyday issue illustrates the difference between an incident and a problem, and the approach to its resolution.

EXAMPLE – INCIDENT AND PROBLEM RESOLUTION

In an office there are many plants that are looked after and watered on a regular basis. However, there is one plant that has leaves that are brown or turning brown. The person looking after the plants just cuts off the brown leaves and waters the plant.

This is just resolving an incident each time it occurs. If nothing else is done, the incident will keep recurring and more and more brown leaves will be cut off.

It is only when a problem management approach is used and the underlying root cause of 'brown leaves' is investigated that the occurrence of these incidents can be understood and prevented. Problem management, rather than just dealing with the effects (i.e. cutting off the brown leaves), looks to determine why the leaves are turning brown.

It is only by analysing the potential underlying root cause(s) of the incidents that their recurrence can be prevented. Therefore, problem management might ask the following questions:

- Is the plant in a hot dry area?
- Is the plant being watered as much or as often as all of the other plants in the office?
- Is the water leaking out of the pot?
- Are the leaves being sprayed as much or as often as all of the other plants in the office?
- Is the plant diseased?

If we check with the person who looks after the plants and confirm that this plant is being treated in exactly the same way as the others, two of the potential causes can be eliminated. If we then examine the pot to see if it is cracked or if there is any evidence of leaking water on the surrounding area, and there is neither, another potential cause can be eliminated. This then means that the underlying cause is likely to be one of the following:

a. The pot is in a hot and dry area.
b. The plant is diseased.

These 'hypotheses' or 'potential causes' now need to be investigated, tested and validated, either by:

1. relocating the plant to another area; or
2. swapping this plant with another, which doesn't suffer from brown leaves, from elsewhere.

The first case (relocating the plant to another more suitable area) will result in either:

- the incidents ceasing completely (cause a); or
- the incidents continuing (cause b).

In contrast, case 2 (swapping this plant with a plant in some other area that doesn't suffer from brown leaves) will result in either:

- the incidents continuing with the original plant in the new location (cause b); or
- the incidents continuing, but with the swapped plant (cause a).

This very simple example demonstrates many problem management methods and techniques, which are described and explained in greater detail in the remainder of this book. It also highlights the difference in focus between the incident management and problem management processes.

Another issue with the implementation of problem management within an organisation is the common misconception that, once a problem management team, problem management targets, procedures and workflow have been established, a successful problem management process has been implemented.

This is not the case. This is probably just the start and not necessarily a good start. All that has been implemented is yet another 'silo'. Problem management should be an organisational capability, a methodology and a way of thinking and acting. It needs to be integrated with many other areas, processes and activities.

3 THE ROLE OF PROBLEM MANAGER

PURPOSE OF THE ROLE

The problem manager role is required within an organisation to coordinate and manage activities related to the resolution of incidents and problems.

Of course, the analysis and resolution of problems should be everyone's concern because all of us from time to time face problems. How we approach and resolve them is important if we want to succeed in our working and personal lives. One of the main roles of a problem manager within an organisation is to provide focus and leadership on problem management techniques, methods and processes. The more consistent the approach used within an organisation to the resolution of problems, the greater the benefit and value of that approach is to the organisation. Problems can be solved more quickly and more easily if everyone in an organisation uses the same approach and the same terminology. This is particularly true where group techniques such as brainstorming are used.

The purpose of the problem manager role and the problem management function is to:

- coordinate, lead, manage and continually improve problem management capability and activities within an organisation.

This means that problem managers need to be seen as the focus for all activities related to the management of issues and problems and their resolution. Therefore the main objectives of the role are to:

- minimise the business disruption caused by incidents and problems on an organisation;

- eliminate recurring incidents and prevent incidents and problems from occurring through root cause analysis and the resolution of problems, wherever it is cost-effective to do so;

- continually improve the problem manager role and the problem management capability within the organisation.

The main activities required of a problem manager to support the purpose and objectives are to:

- periodically review and analyse all incident and problem record types and volumes, identifying trends and 'areas of pain', and triggering consideration of the creation of new problem records;

- manage problems and problem records through their lifecycle, from detection and recording, through classification, prioritisation, assessment, investigation, analysis, possible escalation, resolution, review and closure;

- support all incident management and problem management activities;

- provide a focal point, a point of leadership and coordination of all problem management activities;

- reduce duplicated effort on the root cause analysis (RCA) of incidents and problems;

- improve prioritisation and focus of support effort and resources, based on business impact and need.

The problem management function is also responsible for ensuring effective and efficient coordination and management of problems, including communication to stakeholders on the progress and the estimated time for resolution. These activities, methods and techniques are considered in further detail in the following sections and also in Chapter 4.

There are two distinct aspects to the problem manager role and activities: reactive and proactive.

Reactive aspect

The reactive side of problem management is concerned with identifying, analysing and solving problems, linked to one or more incidents that have previously occurred. So this aspect of problem management involves the analysis of events and incidents that have previously happened and continue to happen. It is principally driven by reacting to events and incidents, creating problem records and managing them through their lifecycle to resolution and closure.

Proactive aspect

Proactive problem management consists of activities and techniques associated with the prevention of avoidable incidents and problems before they occur. This involves taking proactive or pre-emptive action to prevent foreseeable errors and failures. This could be achieved in a number of ways:

- By taking action when changes to normal patterns of activity are detected, thresholds are threatened or warning messages are received.
- By identifying weaknesses in the infrastructure.
- By identifying trends and working to resolve the underlying root cause of incidents and problems.
- By using proactive problem management techniques, such as risk assessment and management or component failure impact analysis (CFIA) to identify and remove areas of weakness or potential areas of failure, before they impact the services, customers and users.

Ultimately these activities should lead to a close working relationship between problem management activities and continual service improvement (CSI) activities. This area is covered in greater detail in 'Continual service improvement' on page 46.

ATTRIBUTES, KNOWLEDGE AND SKILLS

The following three subsections consider the key attributes, knowledge and skills needed to make a good problem manager. It is not necessary for a problem manager to have all of the elements, but generally speaking, the more of them a person has, the better a problem manager they will be.

Attributes

A good problem manager needs the following attributes:

- **To be a good listener** – The ability to listen to people's opinions and see their point of view. This is particularly useful when analysing problems, facilitating meetings or during discussions in brainstorming sessions (page 100).

- **To be open-minded** – An open approach, receptive to new ideas and suggestions, with no preconceptions, especially when trying to consider alternative potential solutions to complex issues and problems.

- **To be analytical** – A systematic approach to problem analysis and resolution, being able to analyse and simplify complex situations and problems is an extremely useful attribute for a problem manager.

- **To be a logical thinker** – The ability to think in a structured and rational way, with the same approach to problem solving – a logical approach to problem solving and an ability to eliminate illogical potential root causes and solutions during the analysis of problems is essential.

- **To be a lateral thinker** – The ability to consider all options and 'think outside the box', particularly when discarding preconceptions and invalid assumptions during the analysis of problems.

- **To be curious** – An inquisitive nature (questioning, but not confrontational) is useful when trying to collect information, evidence and diagnostics when analysing incidents and problems.

- **To be authoritative** – The ability to act with authority, but not in a dictatorial way, is essential when running meetings, deciding, agreeing and allocating actions and timescales with owners.

- **To be impartial** – To act even-handedly without bias and preference when determining and agreeing courses of action and allocating actions to individuals.

- **To be respectful and be respected** – One of the keys to success as a problem manager is the development of good relationships with support teams, suppliers and resolver groups – successful relationships are built on mutual trust and respect.

- **To be a quick learner** – The ability to grasp new ideas, concepts and information and quickly use them to good effect, and to retain information – complex issues often arise during RCA activities, and a problem manager needs to consider many different potential alternatives, often considering conflicting proposed solutions.

- **To be understanding** – The ability to understand people and an audience, and being able to react to them and the situation in order to adapt an approach and technique based on the needs of the circumstances.

- **To be able to step back** – The ability to withdraw from the detail and take the 'helicopter view' of the big picture – when analysing an incident or problem it is often useful to step back from the technical detail in order to develop an approach and identify the most appropriate course of action.

- **To be customer service focused** – The ability to provide a high level of service centred on customer and business outcomes. The ability to understand and align with business and customer needs and priorities is an essential requirement of a problem manager to ensure that the important business and customer issues and problems are given highest priority and are addressed first.

Knowledge

It is important that a problem manager has the knowledge and information to make decisions with regards to assessing the impact and priority of problems and problem records. It is essential that a problem manager has good knowledge of the following:

- **Problem management methods and techniques** – This is especially true of problem analysis techniques. Problem managers need to be able to lead, guide and coach others in the use of these methods and techniques in the resolution of incidents and problems.

- **Service structure and dynamics, and their interdependencies** – Problem managers also need to understand the dependencies of business processes on IT services so that they can accurately assess the business impact of incidents and problems and prioritise their resolution appropriately.

- **Technical aspects** – It is not necessary for a problem manager to have a detailed technical knowledge in any particular area. It is more important that they have a broad knowledge of technology and understanding of how the technology is used in supporting services and business processes. This knowledge is useful in problem analysis, service failure analysis (SFA – see page 120) and component failure impact analysis (CFIA – see page 126).

- **The business** – An awareness of the business units and their use of IT, and the business processes and their dependencies on IT services, will ensure that the problem manager maintains a business focus and acts accordingly. Problem managers should also understand and appreciate the business impact and importance of IT services and activities on customers, users, business processes and activities, so they can accurately assess the business impact and priority for problem analysis and resolution.

- **Stakeholder and customer roles and needs** – This ensures that the problem manager involves the correct people in problem management activities, particularly communication and escalation activities.

- **Users and their use of services** – In order to understand the user's perspective. Also a knowledge of who the 'super users' are for particular business processes and services will ensure that the correct people are involved in the appropriate problem management activities.

- **The organisation and its structure** – Enabling the problem manager to involve the correct business areas in the appropriate problem management activities. A similar knowledge of the IT organisation and its structure is also important for the same reasons.

- **Information** – It is important that a problem manager knows how and where to access all the information necessary for support.

Skills

The following is a list of some of the main skills needed to make a good problem manager.

- **Problem methods and techniques** – One of the principal activities of a problem manager is to use and apply problem management methods and techniques effectively in the management and resolution of problems, so it is absolutely essential that problem managers have this skill and experience. It will also enable them to coach and lead others in the use of problem methods and techniques.

- **Problem analysis** – An essential skill of problem managers is the ability to recognise large and complex problems and to analyse them in a logical, structured manner, breaking them down into simpler, less complex elements or components. Very often complex problems consist of a number of smaller inter-connected problems. If these complex problems can be analysed and broken down into a number of smaller problems, they can be resolved more quickly.

- **Problem solving** – Although problem managers do not normally solve many problems themselves, it is important that they have the skills to analyse and resolve problems. Many problems that occur will be unrelated to specific technology but will relate to people and process issues. These problems should be resolved by problem managers themselves without relying on the technical skills of resolver groups. It is also important that problem managers can lead and coach others in problem solving methods and techniques, especially in the resolution of technically complex problems.

- **Establishing and maintaining good relationships** – Problem managers are dependent upon many different groups, teams and individuals, especially resolver groups. Therefore, the knowledge and skill to develop and maintain good relationships with many different groups and personalities is essential to success as a problem manager.

- **Facilitating** – Problem managers will need to be involved in the conducting and chairing of many meetings. They will need the skill to lead meetings unobtrusively to deliver the correct outcome especially during major incident and major problem review meetings.

- **Enabling** – Problem managers are not usually the resolvers of many problems, therefore, they need the skill to enable, encourage and coach others to resolve problems while trying to identify and resolve the underlying cause of incidents and problems.

- **Resource management** – Many complex problems will often involve the use of many resources and skills. Problem managers will need to be able to manage this virtual team of resources in order to resolve these complex issues and problems efficiently and effectively.

- **Recognition** – Problem managers are dependent upon the support and assistance of many people from many different areas in the resolution of problems, often in demanding and stressful situations. This often requires people to work above and beyond their normal roles to meet tight timescales. When this happens problem managers need to provide positive feedback to people's team leader or manager on their performance and their commitment to problem management activities. They also need to ensure that these people are publically recognised and wherever possible rewarded for their contributions. This will ensure their continued support of the problem management process and activities.

SKILLS FRAMEWORK FOR THE INFORMATION AGE

The Skills Framework for the Information Age (SFIA) is a framework that describes professional skills needed for IT-related roles.[6] SFIA contains the definition of 96 IT-related skills, organised into categories and subcategories for convenience, with each skill defined at one or more of the seven levels. Table 3.1 highlights the Problem Management skill. SFIA can be used to assess and develop one's own capability as well as the capability of others. The framework is also useful for:

- creating and implementing personal development plans for individuals;
- defining roles and responsibilities of personnel when establishing or improving a capability within an organisation;
- assessing the consistency of job and role definitions across many different IT practices and disciplines.

---

[6] SFIA (2011) SFIA 5 Framework reference. SFIA Foundation

21

Table 3.1 The categories of SFIA

Category	Sub-category	Skill		SFIA levels							
			Code	1	2	3	4	5	6	7	
Strategy and architecture	(4)	(23)									
Business change	(4)	(20)									
Solution development and implementation	(3)	(18)									
Service management	Service strategy										
Service management	Service design										
Service management	Service transition										
Service management	Service operation	System software	SYSP								
Service management	Service operation	System administration	SCAD								

(Continued)

Table 3.1 (Continued)

Category	Sub-category	Skill	Code	SFIA levels						
				1	2	3	4	5	6	7
Service management	Service operation	Radio frequency engineering	RFEN							
Service management	Service operation	Applications support	ASUP							
Service management	Service operation	IT operations	ITOP							
Service management	Service operation	Database administration	DBAD							
Service management	Service operation	Storage management	STMG							
Service management	Service operation	Network support	NTAS							
Service management	**Service operation**	**Problem management**	**PBMG**			✓	✓	✓		

(Continued)

Table 3.1 (Continued)

Category	Sub-category	Skill	SFIA levels							
			Code	1	2	3	4	5	6	7
Service management	Service operation	Service desk and incident management	USUP							
Service management	Service operation	IT estate management	DCMA							
Procurement and management support	(2)	(9)								
Client interface	(2)	(5)								

Problem management is one of the 11 skills contained within the service operation sub-category of the service management category of SFIA. Each of the skills is mapped to an appropriate range of the seven levels of responsibility contained within SFIA (see Table 3.2).

Table 3.2 The seven levels of responsibility of SFIA

SFIA levels

Level 7 **Set strategy, inspire, mobilise:** with overall authority and responsibility for a significant area, defines strategy, influences at the highest levels with strategic relationships

Level 6 **Initiate, influence:** policies and plans, within a defined area of authority and responsibility, with influential relationships, contributing to strategy and performing highly complex activities

Level 5 **Ensure, advise:** influences all areas, building effective relationships, performing a variety of complex activities

Level 4 **Enable:** by influencing specialist peers and customers, performing a range of complex activities, including analysing and resolving complex problems

Level 3 **Apply:** skills and influences other team members, performing a broad range of tasks, using a logical approach to the definition and resolution of problems

Level 2 **Assist:** others in performing a wide variety of tasks, including contributing to the resolution of routine tasks

Level 1 **Follow:** documented processes and procedures and perform routine tasks

---

These levels of responsibility are each defined in terms of autonomy, complexity, influence and business skills. The higher the level of the skill within SFIA, the greater the capability required in these terms. Several SFIA skills will be required by a problem manager, including the problem management skill, which is defined at levels 3, 4, and 5, and can be summarised as:

- Problem management (Level 3)
  - Investigates problems in systems and services.
  - Assists with the implementation of agreed problem reduction and resolution activities and actions.
- Problem management (Level 4)
  - Instigates and monitors the progress of problem resolution activities.
  - Assists with the implementation of agreed problem reduction and resolution activities and actions.
- Problem management (Level 5)
  - Ensures that actions to investigate, and resolve problems are progressed.
  - Ensures that action is taken to investigate, progress and resolve problems.
  - Ensures that problems are appropriately documented within the problem management system.
  - Analyses incident and problem trends.
  - Coordinates the implementation of problem reduction and resolution actions.

SFIA*plus* activities

SFIA*plus* is a tool based on the SFIA skills framework and the Industry Structure Model (ISM). It is a framework and model against which people's roles and skills can be reviewed and evaluated. It also enables career progression plans to be developed together with individual training and development plans to support them. This allows organisations to tailor roles and responsibilities to meet the needs of individuals working in their organisation.

Information on the activities of the different levels of problem management roles is also provided within SFIA*plus*. The following is a summary of the information at each of these levels.

- Level 3 activities
  - Investigates problems, process and services.
  - Assists with the implementation of agreed problem reduction and resolution activities and actions, in conjunction with the service desk, change management and service asset and configuration management (SACM).
  - Matches incident records against existing problem and known error records, and other incident records.
  - Updates incident and problem records within the incident and problem management systems.
  - Monitors the impact of problems on agreed service levels with service level management (SLM).
  - Assists with the production of problem management reports.
  - Completes problem investigation, progression and resolution actions within agreed timescales.
- Level 4 activities
  - Instigates and monitors the progress of problem resolution activities.
  - Assists with the implementation of agreed problem reduction and resolution activities and actions, coordinating the activities of resolver groups, in conjunction with the service desk, incident management, change management and SACM.
  - Reviews and documents incidents and problems within the incident and problem management systems.

- Matches incident records with existing problem and known error records, and other incident records.
- Monitors the impact of problems on agreed service levels with SLM.
- Assists with the production of problem management reports, including:
  1. the analysis and review of incident and problem trends to identify and take action on potential problem areas, to improve problem management and minimise the impact of incidents and problems;
  2. the achievement of problem management targets in line with agreed service levels.
- Completes problem investigation, progression and resolution actions within agreed timescales.
- Ensures that incidents, problems and known errors identified in test and development activities are recorded, accessible and understood.
- Instigates proactive improvements by identifying and analysing issues with services, components processes and activities.
- Provides advice and guidance on problem management methods and activities.

- Level 5 activities
  - Manages rapid response, progress and resolution of problems, thereby minimising the business disruption caused by incidents and problems.
  - Ensures that problems are appropriately managed and documented within the problem management system and coordinates the use of workarounds and requests for change (RFCs).
  - Ensures that up-to-date information is maintained on major problems and appropriate communication is made to all relevant parties.
  - Proactively matches incident records with existing problem and known error records, and other incident records.

- Monitors the impact of problems on agreed service levels with SLM.

- Instigates and monitors the implementation of problem reductions and resolutions, in conjunction with the service desk, incident management, change management and SACM.

- Ensures that incidents, problems and known errors identified in test and development activities are recorded, accessible and understood.

- Ensures that problem investigation, progression and resolution actions are completed within agreed timescales.

- Ensures that the suitable reports are produced and that the relevant people and groups are appropriately informed of services, service issues and service levels.

- Continually endeavours to improve the problem management process, techniques and activities by:

  1. identifying and instigating proactive improvements by identifying and analysing issues with services, components, processes and activities;
  2. instigating and monitoring improvement plans and strategies, including proactive problem management activities;
  3. analysing incident and problem trends;
  4. reviewing problem analysis, reduction and resolution activities;
  5. assessing and reviewing the root causes of incidents and problems;
  6. reviewing problem management systems and tools.

- Makes decisions and revises actions, based on problem management reports and information.

An organisation can use this information to:

- review and assess individual's roles within an organisation;

- develop individual's skills and capabilities within a particular area;
- develop individual's training plans;
- tailor job or role descriptions to meet the specific needs of the organisation.

ROLES AND RESPONSIBILITIES

This section describes a number of roles and responsibilities that need to be performed to operate an effective problem management process within an organisation.

ITIL roles and responsibilities

ITIL is probably the most widely used framework within the IT industry. It provides comprehensive guidelines on the key practices and processes needed for effective IT services. The problem management process is covered in the ITIL *Service Operation* book.

In ITIL, some of the roles in the area of problem management are described in terms of a set of activities, whereas others are described in terms of a set of generic activities and a set of specific activities. Where the activities are generic, they are relevant for all processes, not just the problem management process, whereas the specific activities relate purely to the problem management process.

Problem management process owner

This role is responsible for owning problem management and ensuring that the process is suitable and appropriate to the organisation.

In some organisations the role is combined with that of the problem management process manager and assigned to a single person. In other organisations the roles are assigned to separate people. Another approach used by some organisations is to combine the role of the problem management process owner with the process owner role for other processes. For example one person might be made responsible for the ownership of the event, incident and problem management processes, so that a fully integrated approach could be adopted to the design and implementation of these three processes.

The role consists of generic process manager activities, plus specific activities of a problem management process owner.

The specific activities of a problem management process owner are:

- coordinating design activities between problem management and other processes to ensure that effective interfaces are implemented and automated;
- planning and maintaining a set of problem models and workflows.

The generic activities of a problem management process owner are:

- working with service owners, process owners and managers to coordinate process interfaces and activities and ensure service levels are maintained;
- defining, reviewing and revising the problem management process strategy, policy and standards;
- promoting, instigating and coordinating the design, change, measurement, effectiveness, review, compliance, audit and improvement of the problem management process;
- ensuring that adequate and appropriate resources, documentation and information are made available to support all problem management activities and process needs;
- ensuring that all personnel involved in problem management activities have the capability, knowledge and access to the appropriate information to understand and perform their process role;

- identifying and reviewing issues and opportunities associated with the problem management process and instigating potential improvements to the process – subsequently, working in conjunction with the CSI manager and the problem management process owner, to review and prioritise improvements.

- raising the awareness of the problem management process and ensuring that all personnel are made aware of the importance of the process and any changes made to the process.

Problem management process manager

This role is responsible for the day-to-day operation and management of the problem management process. In some organisations the role is combined with that of the problem management process owner and assigned to a single person.

Again, the role consists of generic activities performed by all process managers and the specific activities of a problem management process manager.

The specific activities of a problem management process manager are:

- managing and planning problem management resource levels, tools and tool support;

- liaising with problem resolver groups and suppliers to ensure they fulfil their obligations contained within agreements and contracts, with respect to problem management activities and information;

- ensuring and improving the accuracy of problem records and information;

- ensuring and improving, the accuracy and use of the known errors, the known error database (KEDB) and the associated searching procedures;

- conducting major problem reviews and reports and managing resulting actions.

The generic activities of a problem management process manager are:

- working with service owners, process owners and managers to coordinate process interfaces and activities and ensure service levels are maintained;

- managing and coordinating process activities, roles and resources throughout the service lifecycle;

- monitoring, measuring and improving process performance;

- identifying and reviewing issues and opportunities associated with the problem management process and instigating potential improvements to the process. Subsequently, working in conjunction with the CSI manager and the problem management process owner, to review and prioritise improvements.

Problem management practitioner role

ITIL lists a generic process practitioner role, which refers to an individual working on one or more problem activities, generally under supervision and guidance of someone, such as the problem management process owner. The typical responsibilities of this generic role are:

- understanding how their role contributes to the overall delivery of service and creation of value for the business;

- performing one or more process activities, such as:

  - updating records to log the correct progression of activities;

  - confirming activity inputs, outputs and interfaces are correct;

  - ensuring that their stakeholder contributions are effective.

33

Problem manager

In this book the term 'problem manager' is used as a generic term for someone working at some level within the problem management process. This role is referred to within ITIL, but no role is explicitly defined. It implies a role, with authority, that is responsible for managing and progressing problem records through their lifecycle and the resolution of problems. There is an implication that the following activities form part of a problem manager role:

- Acting as a point of escalation when agreed problem analysis or resolution tasks or actions are not completed within their agreed timescale.

- Applying problem management techniques.

- Managing and coordinating root cause analysis of problems and incidents.

- Assisting with resolution of the root cause of incidents and problems.

- Escalating and communicating with appropriate team leaders or managers.

- Facilitating major problem review meetings.

- Entering and validating 'lessons learnt' articles, knowledge articles, known error records and workarounds into the KEDB or SKMS, ensuring that relevant search key categories and criteria are correctly used.

Problem analyst

The problem analyst is typically responsible for performing a number of problem management activities, especially ensuring that problem resolution resources are coordinated and used effectively in the resolution of problems and incidents. The typical specific activities of this role are:

- reviewing and analysing incident data and related problems and coordinating problem activity and resolutions;

- investigating and progressing the analysis and resolution of problems;
- instigating RFCs to resolve the root cause of problems;
- reviewing the prioritisation and classification of problems;
- updating known error and workaround information within the KEDB, monitoring problems, and ensuring that incident management staff are aware of existing known errors and workarounds;
- assisting with major incidents and the identification of root causes.

Other potential responsibilities for problem managers

A problem manager might also perform the following activities and have the following responsibilities:

- Assisting with the management and coordination of major incidents in conjunction with the service desk and incident management. Problem managers often have useful skills, attributes and expertise to make significant contributions to the management of major incidents. This includes the coaching and mentoring of service desk and incident management personnel.

- The proactive prevention of potential failure events and incidents from occurring or recurring. This could include working with any groups, but is particularly applicable to personnel from the service desk, incident management, event management or any of the support groups or resolver groups.

- The recruitment, management, training etc. of staff, especially those involved in problem management activities. This might include personnel from the service desk, incident management or resolver groups.

- Contributing as required to the change advisory board (CAB). This could include the sponsorship of RFCs, explaining the reasons for failed changes or advising on the adverse impact of changes.

- Continually reviewing the problem management procedures to improve their effectiveness and efficiency.

- Facilitating 'post-mortem' reviews on the effectiveness of incident and problem resolution etc. – especially the resolution of major incidents and problems.

- Keeping aware of the business use of IT in order to prioritise correctly areas for service improvements or problems for analysis and resolution, based on business impact and value.

- Identifying incidents and problems with high impact on the business, high cost etc. and initiating and undertaking service and process improvement programmes, where appropriate.

RACI chart for problem management

Each organisation should determine the accountability and responsibility for its problem management activities. The best way of visualising this is with a RACI chart, in which the characters R, A, C and I are used to indicate the responsibility of individuals within process activities as follows:

R – responsible

A – accountable

C – consulted

I – informed

An example of a RACI chart for the problem management activities is shown in Table 3.3. It shows an example of the involvement of the problem management roles and other related areas within the problem management activities.

Table 3.3 Example RACI chart for problem management activities

Problem management activity	Problem management process owner	Problem management process manager	Problem manager	Problem analyst	Problem management practitioner	Resolver groups	Service desk	Incident management	Event management	Change management
Problem process design	AR	R	C	C	C	C	C	C	C	C
Problem detection		AR	R	R	R	R	R	R	R	—
Identification and creation of problem records		AR	R	R	R	R	—	—	—	—
Categorisation of problems		AR	R	R	R	C	—	—	—	—
Prioritisation of problems		AR	R	R	R	C	—	—	—	—
Investigation and diagnosis of problems		AR	R	R	R	R	—	—		

(Continued)

Table 3.3 (Continued)

Problem management activity	Problem management process owner	Problem management process manager	Problem manager	Problem analyst	Problem management practitioner	Resolver groups	Service desk	Incident management	Event management	Change management
Creating workarounds		AR	R	R	R	R	—	—		
Raising known errors		R	R	R	R	R	—	—		
Resolution of problems		R	R	R	R	R	—	—		
Closing problems			R	R	R		—	—		
Completion of major problem reviews		AR	R				—	—		
Monitoring progress of problems and known errors		AR	R	R	R	—	—	—		

(Continued)

Table 3.3 (Continued)

Problem management activity	Problem management process owner	Problem management process manager	Problem manager	Problem analyst	Problem management practitioner	Resolver groups	Service desk	Incident management	Event management	Change management
Measurement and reporting of the process	C	AR	R	R	R	I	I	I	I	I
Improvement of the process	AR	R	R	R	R	R	R	R	R	R
Day-to-day operation of the process	C	AR	R	R	R	R	R	R	R	
Review and audit the problem process	AR	R	C	C	C	C	C	C	C	C

Key: A – accountable, R – responsible, C – consulted, I – Informed

INTERFACES AND DEPENDENCIES

In too many organisations problem management is a process 'silo', working in isolation from other processes. The more mature problem management processes interface and integrate with many other areas and processes, and this section considers some of the key areas and processes for the problem manager to consider for integrating the problem management process, as shown in Figure 3.1.

When implementing a problem management process within an organisation, not all of these interfaces should be implemented from the start. A small number of the most important interfaces for the organisation should be identified and prioritised for implementation first. These should be the interfaces that deliver the most increased value to the business and customers. The most important interfaces will vary dependent upon the needs of the business and the organisation, however they will almost certainly include the interfaces to the service desk and incident management.

The interface needs to be considered as bidirectional. This means that not only will problem management require information and assistance from other areas and processes, but it should also provide information and assistance to other areas.

Service desk and incident management

The service desk is the single point of contact for all service users. The service desk staff are therefore one of the main users of the incident management process. Incident management is the process for managing incidents from detection through to resolution and closure. The interface and interworking between problem management, and the service desk and incident management is probably the most important interface to focus on because of the mutual dependency of the two processes, and its efficient operation is vitally important to both the incident management and the problem management

Figure 3.1 The key problem management interfaces

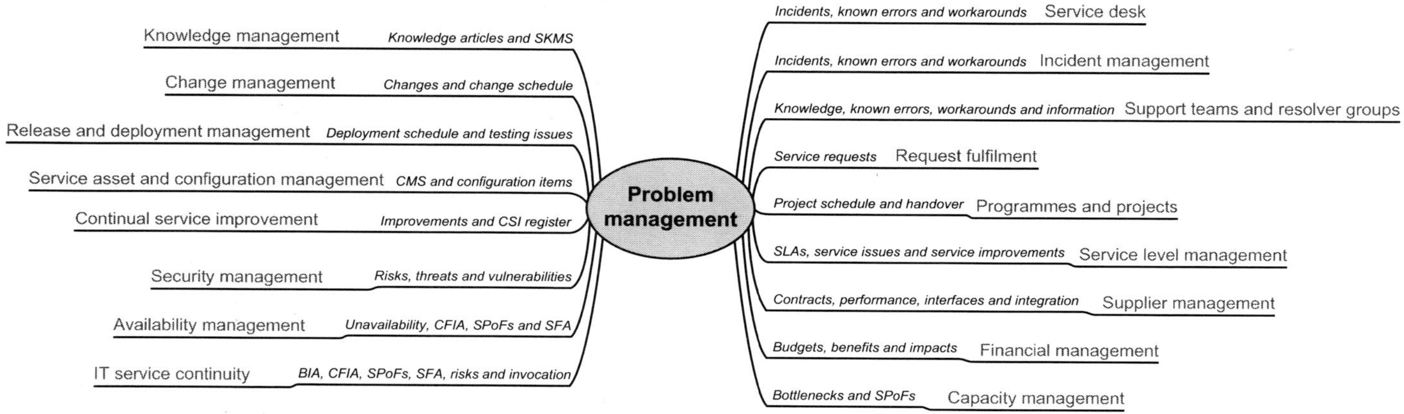

Problem management

- Knowledge management — *Knowledge articles and SKMS*
- Change management — *Changes and change schedule*
- Release and deployment management — *Deployment schedule and testing issues*
- Service asset and configuration management — *CMS and configuration items*
- Continual service improvement — *Improvements and CSI register*
- Security management — *Risks, threats and vulnerabilities*
- Availability management — *Unavailability, CFIA, SPoFs and SFA*
- IT service continuity — *BIA, CFIA, SPoFs, SFA, risks and invocation*

- *Incidents, known errors and workarounds* — Service desk
- *Incidents, known errors and workarounds* — Incident management
- *Knowledge, known errors, workarounds and information* — Support teams and resolver groups
- *Service requests* — Request fulfilment
- *Project schedule and handover* — Programmes and projects
- *SLAs, service issues and service improvements* — Service level management
- *Contracts, performance, interfaces and integration* — Supplier management
- *Budgets, benefits and impacts* — Financial management
- *Bottlenecks and SPoFs* — Capacity management

processes. This is why it is essential that this interface is considered a top priority for most organisations.

Good problem management is heavily dependent upon the quality and capability of:

- the staff working within the incident management process;
- the incident management process;
- the information from the incident management process.

The effectiveness of all of the reactive activities of problem management is totally dependent upon these three aspects, particularly the incident management information.

The key interactions between the main areas involved in the resolution of incidents and problems are illustrated in Figure 3.2. The key interactions for problem management are shown in solid lines and the key interactions for the service desk and incident management are shown in dotted lines.

Figure 3.2 The service desk, incident management and problem management

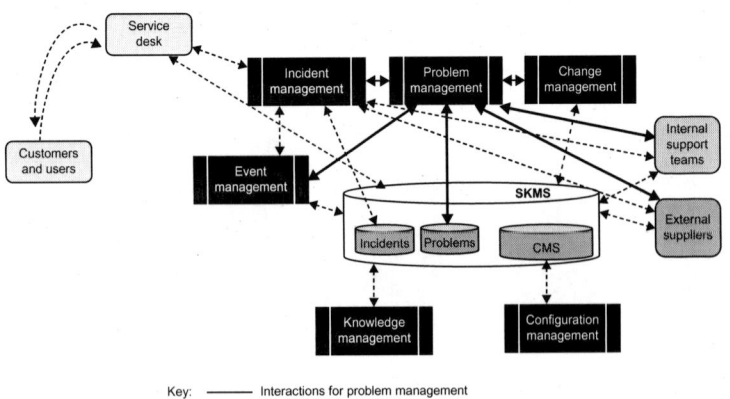

The service desk provides a single point of contact for customers and users. The service desk analysts are principally dependent upon the service desk tool for support and automation, and upon incident management for an effective and efficient incident process and system. These will be the significant things that drive service desk activities. Problem management is responsible for ensuring that the problem management process, activities and system work efficiently with the service desk and incident management processes, activities and systems. Integration and automated interfaces are vital to the smooth operation of these three areas, and their effectiveness will be significantly improved if all resolver groups, support teams and the relevant suppliers also have access to these processes and systems.

The following subsections describe the areas for interworking between the service desk, incident management and problem management.

Incident records and information

The quality and accuracy of the information logged within incident records in the incident management system is crucial to the success of problem management activities. Many of the problem activities, particularly the creation and analysis of problem records, are totally dependent upon the quality of the incident information. Therefore problem managers should work closely with service desk and incident management staff to ensure that the information recorded is accurate, timely and consistent across incident records. Incident management is generally responsible for incident records and information.

Known errors and workarounds

Vital areas of information provided to incident management and service desk staff by problem management are the known errors and workarounds. Known errors and workarounds should be recorded in either a known error database (KEDB) or a service knowledge management system (SKMS), if one exists. The quality of the information within these records and the ability to locate that information are crucial to the quality of service provided by the service desk. Many incidents can be quickly resolved if they can be matched with other incidents, known errors and workarounds, providing rapid resolution of customer and user issues. Problem management is generally responsible for known errors and workarounds.

Incident categorisation

The categorisation of incidents needs to work effectively for both the incident and problem management activities. It is essential for incident management that incidents can be quickly compared with and matched to other incidents and problems. However, problem management also needs incident categories to work for them in the analysis, trending and reporting of incidents and problems, so that they can focus on the key issues causing most disruption to the business. This will enable problem managers to prioritise the analysis, processing and resolution of problems. It is most effective when incident and problem categories are similar, consistent or even the same. Service desk, incident management and problem management should work together to ensure that the incident categorisation mechanism works effectively for the three areas.

Incident matching

This is a major area of interaction between the service desk, incident management and problem management. It is the ability of service desk staff to match new incidents to existing or similar incidents or problems rapidly. The more incidents that can be matched to other incidents, problems and known errors, the quicker and the better the response provided to the end user. The best way of achieving this is for the incident management system to search the incident and problem records automatically for matching records as new incidents are being created. If any are found, the best matches can be presented to the agent logging the new incident record. The agent can then associate this incident with any appropriately matching records and hopefully provide a resolution for the user. Service desk, incident management and problem management should work together to ensure that incident matching works effectively for all areas.

User and customer communication

All user and customer communication should be coordinated and performed by the service desk as a central point of focus and contact. Problem managers should ensure that appropriate and timely communication is performed through the service desk for all problem issues.

Knowledge articles and the service knowledge management system

Both incident and problem management will gain considerable benefit from sharing knowledge articles in a single knowledge management repository – the service knowledge management system (SKMS) – in particular from sharing known errors, workarounds and the lessons learnt from major incident and major problem reviews. The more knowledge that is shared between the two processes, the more effective and efficient both processes will be. Knowledge management should own the SKMS and the knowledge articles contained within the SKMS.

Assisting with major incidents

Problem managers can often be of great value in assisting the service desk with the management and progression of major incidents. Many of the attributes and skills of a problem manager are useful in the management of major incidents. For example, the skills required to conduct a major problem review are equally applicable to conducting a review of a major incident. Incident management is generally responsible for the management of major incidents.

Management information

Sharing reports and management information between the service desk, incident management and problem management can provide great benefit and increased effectiveness in all three areas. They all need to work together to ensure that the information and the reports are accurate and consistent.

Reduction of incidents and problems

All three areas need to aim to reduce the overall number and impact of incidents and problems. This can only be achieved in an effective way if all three areas work together closely.

Development issues

All three areas should work together to ensure that all defects, incidents, known errors, problems, knowledge articles, issues and experiences from development and testing environments are used to minimise the issues experienced by users with the live services. This will improve the quality of the service delivered to service customers and users.

Incident and problem arbitration

The service desk, incident management and problem management need to work together to minimise situations where there is discussion and disagreement on the responsibility for the investigation, diagnosis and resolution of incidents and problems. Arbitration is the responsibility of problem management, and problem managers should work quickly to intervene, arbitrate and resolve these discussions and disputes in order to reduce delays and duplicated or wasted effort.

Improving the service desk experience

All three areas should work together to improve service desk experience, both in terms of quality and speed. This activity should particularly include improving the experience, the value and the usage of the service desk self-help service. This will not only improve the effectiveness of all three areas, but more importantly will improve the customer and user experience. The service desk is responsible for the effectiveness and quality of the service desk experience. More information on this aspect of the service desk experience is contained in Chapter 4.

Continual service improvement

The purpose of the continual service improvement (CSI) process is to manage and successfully implement service improvements through their lifecycle. It is very important that there is a close link between the CSI process and problem management. Good problem managers consider every problem an opportunity for improvement, and, therefore, it is important that wherever possible problem manager(s) work closely with the CSI manager or the person who is ultimately responsible for the success of all CSI activities. This will help problem managers to develop a culture of positive, proactive capability. For this reason, in some organisations the problem manager and CSI manager roles are combined, with the following responsibilities.

- **Opportunities for improvement** – The analysis of problems and incidents offer the perfect chance to identify opportunities for improvement. Wherever possible problem managers should use these opportunities to identify and register improvement suggestions. Wherever possible improvements should be instigated that reduce business disruption caused by incidents and problems. All improvement suggestions should be recorded in a central CSI register.

- **Prioritisation of improvements** – Problem managers should work closely with the CSI manager, service owners and service managers to help prioritise those improvements that are likely to have the greatest potential benefit and value to the business, customers and users, through the resolution and removal of problems and potential incidents.

- **CSI register** – Problem managers should use the CSI register as a means of instigating and implementing improvements that resolve, remove or prevent problems and potential incidents or reduce the business disruption caused by them.

Change management

The purpose of change management is to control changes through their lifecycle and ensure minimum disruption caused by the implementation of changes. The link between problem management and change management is an important one. It is a part of both aspects of problem management: the reactive aspect (i.e. reporting on failed changes) and the proactive one (i.e. providing input on the potential impact of proposed changes). The following lists the main areas of interaction.

- **The change schedule** – This is a very important reference point for problem managers. It should be one of the first things checked when analysing specific problems or incidents because in many organisations one of the biggest causes of incidents and problems is failed changes.

- **Change requests** – Problem managers should raise requests for change (RFCs) for all problem resolutions requiring changes to configuration items (CIs) or items under the control of change management. Unauthorised changes often fail and are again the cause of many incidents and problems.

- **Failed changes** – Problem managers need to work closely with change management on the management of failed changes, particularly concerning reports and feedback on the impact of failed changes. They should also work together to reduce the volume and the impact of failed changes.

- **Change advisory board (CAB)** – Problem management should be represented at the CAB to report on failed changes and to provide feedback on the potential impact of proposed changes.

Release and deployment management

The purpose of release and deployment management is to plan, schedule and deploy new releases into the live environment, while protecting existing services. As well as working closely with change management, problem managers should also be involved with the release and deployment management process to ensure smooth transition of new releases into the live environment, by focusing on:

- **Release schedules** – Problem managers should have access to the proposed release schedules at all times so that they are aware of all major release dates.

- **Deploying problem resolutions** – Problem managers should use the release and deployment management process to deploy problem resolutions into the live environment.

- **Development and testing issues** – Problem managers should ensure that defects, known errors, workarounds and issues experienced within development and testing activities are transferred into the KEDB and the SKMS and used to minimise the impact of new releases into the live environment.

- **Handover** – Often problems occur within organisations around the use of service acceptance criteria (SAC) and handover procedures. Problem managers should work with release and deployment management to minimise the issues and problems in this area by establishing effective SAC and handover procedures that are simple, appropriate and automated wherever possible.

- **Post-release problems** – A common cause of problems is the 'surge' in the number of incidents and problems occurring in the period just after the deployment of a new release. Figure 3.3 illustrates this situation for the customer relationship management (CRM) service. It shows a massive 'surge' in the total number of incidents recorded per week after two releases (R3.1 and R3.2). Analysis of this 'surge of post-release' incidents showed that many of the incidents were caused by either a lack of information and knowledge of the users or insufficient testing of the release. These two areas were significantly addressed in later releases, such that from release R3.3 onwards, both the post-release 'surge' and the level of incidents were reduced, even though some of these later releases were significantly larger than the earlier releases.

Figure 3.3 The release and deployment 'surge'

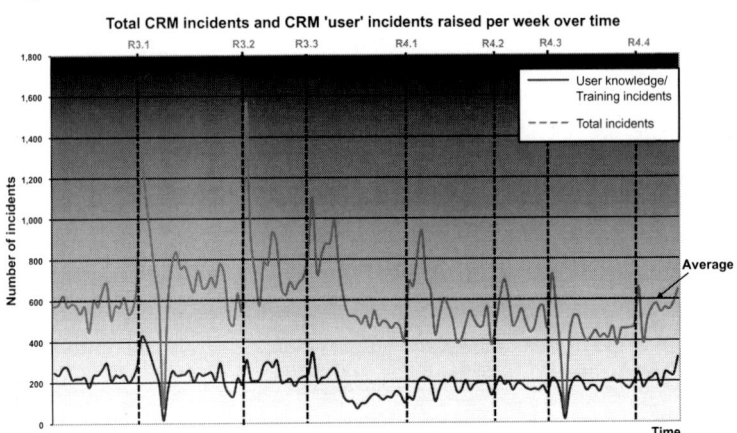

Total CRM incidents and CRM 'user' incidents raised per week over time

Service assets and configuration management

The purpose of service asset and configuration management (SACM) is to ensure that the assets required to deliver services are managed and that accurate information is available on those assets. In order to achieve this, SACM should maintain a configuration management system (CMS). The CMS is a valuable source of information for all areas. It should contain details of all the assets or CIs used within an organisation for the delivery of services, together with the relationships between them. Problem managers should use the CMS for:

- **Identifying faulty CIs** – Linking incidents, problems, known errors and workarounds to CIs can help to improve the speed of resolution of incidents and problems. Also identifying CIs with a high number of linked incidents and problems enables problem managers to identify failing CIs and other areas of service weakness.

- **Impact assessments of problem resolutions** – Problem managers can use the CMS and CIs to assess the impact of problem resolutions, proactive measures and other improvements before instigating or approving them.

- **Assessments** – Problem managers can use the information in the CMS to simplify the completion of component failure impact assessments (CFIA), single points of failure (SPoFs) reviews and service failure analysis (SFA) assessments.

- **CMS information quality** – Problem managers should assist the service asset and configuration manager by helping to check the accuracy of the information contained within the CMS. This can be achieved by reporting any inconsistencies detected during problem management activities. This will improve the accuracy of the CMS information for the benefit of all areas including problem management.

Knowledge management

The purpose of knowledge management is to share knowledge and information and ensure that these are made available to facilitate informed decision making in all areas. Knowledge management and problem management should work together to ensure that all knowledge articles and lessons learnt from the problem management activities are accurately recorded within the SKMS. However, they also need to ensure that all areas can subsequently find these items easily, and rapidly access and use the information they contain by working together in the following areas:

- **SKMS** – Problem managers should assist the knowledge management process by helping to check the accuracy of the information contained within the SKMS and reporting any inconsistencies. This particularly relates to information held in known error and workaround records and their links with problem records.

- **Lessons learnt** – This information should be held in the SKMS and relates principally to the lessons learnt from major incident and major problem reviews, although it should also include lessons learnt from all other areas as well, for example programmes and projects.

- **Accessibility** – Working together to ensure that information is generally accessible and is categorised and indexed with comprehensive search facilities, so that it can be easily located.

IT security management

The purpose of IT security management is to align IT security with business security, ensuring that all assets are protected and that risks are appropriately managed. Security classification and risk assessment procedures used by problem management and IT security management should be consistent. It is important that IT security management are rapidly made aware of any security incidents or problems as soon as they occur, in order that the impact of any security issues is minimised by focusing on:

- **Security incidents and problems** – Problem managers should ensure that there is a process in place to inform IT security management of all incidents and problems that impact or could potentially impact the security of services and information. Problem managers should also ensure that reports and trends of the types and volumes of security incidents and problems are made available.

- **Risk assessments** – The results of any risk assessments conducted by problem managers should be made available.

- **Security threats and vulnerabilities** – Any security threats, vulnerabilities, weaknesses or single points of failure (SPoFs) identified during problem management activities should be highlighted to IT security management.

Request fulfilment

The purpose of the request fulfilment process is to manage service requests through their lifecycle. Problem management should work together with the request fulfilment process to ensure that the request fulfilment process meets the expectations of the customers and users, by working together on:

- **Incidents and problems** – Analysing and resolving incidents and problems associated with the processing of service requests.

- **Request targets** – Analysing issues associated with service requests that are not being fulfilled within their agreed fulfilment targets and instigating improvements.

- **Self-service requests** – Reviewing and acting upon issues associated with the use of the self-service, service request system and their resolution.

Capacity management

The purpose of the capacity management process is to ensure that the capacity of IT services meets the requirements of the customers in a cost-effective and timely manner. Capacity management should ensure that problem management is made aware of any potential service performance or capacity issues. Capacity management and problem management should work together to ensure that the business impact of any service capacity or performance issues is minimised by sharing information on:

- **Poor service performance** – Problem managers should provide capacity management with information on the types, volumes and trends of incidents and problems relating to poor service performance. Capacity management should make problem management aware of any potential areas of concern that might affect service performance.

- **Problem resolutions** – Problem managers should ensure that the impact of changes and proactive improvements proposed for problem resolution are assessed by capacity management for their impact on service performance.

- **Bottlenecks** – Problem managers should ensure that capacity management is made aware of any potential service and component bottlenecks or SPoFs identified by problem management activities.

Availability management

The purpose of the availability management process is to ensure that the level of service availability delivered meets agreed availability targets in a cost-effective and timely manner. Availability management should work closely with problem management to ensure that the impact of all unavailability events is minimised by regularly reviewing the following:

- **Service unavailability** – Problem managers should provide availability management with information on the types, volumes and trends of incidents and problems relating to service unavailability or component downtime. They can then work together to improve the service availability levels delivered to customers and users.

- **Increasing service availability** – Problem managers should work closely with availability management to identify proactively, as well as reactively, potential opportunities for improving service availability.

- **Assessments and reviews** – Problem managers should work with availability management when completing CFIAs, SPoF reviews, SFAs and risk analysis assessments. This will ensure that duplicated and wasted effort is reduced and there is consistent operation between the two areas.

IT financial management

The purpose of the IT financial management process is to ensure that an appropriate level of funding is obtained to design and deliver services that meet the strategy of the organisation. Problem managers should work with IT financial management to ensure their financial activities are consistent with wider financial policies and procedures. They need to have an awareness and appreciation of the finances in the following areas:

- **Financial impact** – Problem managers should agree the methods and calculations for determining the financial impact of incidents and problems and the values used in pain value analysis. This will ensure that the process and values used are consistent with other financial procedures.

- **Financial benefits** – The cost and financial benefits of proposed problem resolutions and workarounds should be agreed with financial management.

- **Budgets** – The budgets required by problem activities should be agreed and secured with financial management to ensure that adequate funding is available for problem management activities.

IT service continuity management

The purpose of the service continuity management process is to support business continuity management requirements ensuring that risks are managed and agreed minimum service levels can always be delivered. The assessment techniques used by IT service continuity management and problem management should be consistent, with reports and information being shared between the two areas. This will ensure that there is no duplication or wasted effort and that activities are compatible and integrated:

- **Assessments** – Problem managers should work with service continuity management when completing business impact analyses (BIAs), CFIAs, SPoF reviews, SFAs and risk analysis assignments to ensure consistency of operation between the two areas.

• **Invocation** – Problem managers should make themselves familiar with service continuity invocation procedures and plans because they may need to invoke recovery plans when involved in the management of major incidents and major problems.

Supplier management

The purpose of the supplier management process is to ensure that all supplier contracts and services support the needs of the business and that suppliers meet their contractual commitments. This means that the following issues should be regularly reviewed and acted upon by both problem managers and supplier managers:

• **Supplier issues** – Problem managers should ensure that incidents and problems related to suppliers, supplied services and contracts are analysed, reported and trended, and made available to supplier managers and supplier management staff to ensure that any issues are raised during supplier review meetings.

• **Supplier performance** – Issues with regards to suppliers and supplied services not meeting their targets, or meeting targets but not customer expectations, should be made available to supplier managers, and supplier management staff. Improvement actions and plans can be agreed with suppliers.

• **Supplier interfaces** – Interface issues (including incidents and problems with interfaces between suppliers) should be analysed and rectified jointly with supplier management. (For example, incidents and problems being bounced between suppliers, or other resolver groups, with no one accepting responsibility.)

- **Supplier integration** – Issues, incidents and problems with the integration of suppliers' processes and tools should be analysed and rectified jointly with supplier management. (For example, problems being lost during transfer between suppliers, or problems and incidents having to be cut from one supplier's system and pasted into another supplier's system when manual interfaces are used.)

Service level management

The purpose of the service level management process is to ensure that current and planned services are delivered to agreed achievable targets. Problem managers need to ensure that service level managers are provided with information on all major problems and incidents affecting customers and their use of services. This ensures that service managers are adequately briefed for service review meetings with customers. Service level managers need to ensure that problem managers are aware of customer's needs and business impacts and priorities. Therefore the two areas should regularly discuss the following information:

- **Service issues** – Problem managers should ensure that service reports are made available on incidents and problems impacting the level of service delivery for all services, so that these can be discussed in service review meetings.

- **Major issues** – Summary details of major incidents and major problems and their resolution should be made available for service level managers to include in service reports.

- **Service improvements** – Problem managers should discuss proactive service improvements with service level management. Service level management should provide customer and user feedback on the impact of problems and the business benefits of proposed problem workarounds and resolutions and other proactive improvements.

Programmes and projects

The functions responsible for the management of programmes and projects need to work closely with problem managers to ensure smooth and consistent handover of new or changed services into the live environment. This is often an area of 'pain' for many organisations. The main information exchanges required are:

- **Project schedules** – Problem managers should have access to the proposed project schedules at all times so that they are aware of all major project milestone and delivery dates.

- **Project handover issues** – Problem managers need to work with programme and project managers to identify quickly project issues, incidents and problems. From this 'lessons learnt', problem resolutions and improvements should be identified and progressed where necessary. Common causes of problems for discussion in this area are:

  - poor requirements analysis resulting in services not aligned to business needs;
  - a lack of focus on service value and outcomes;
  - no allowance is made for increases in operational budgets or resources within programmes and projects;
  - a lack of documentation, information and knowledge is provided on the new or changed service;
  - a lack of operational resource involvement resulting in poor knowledge transfer to operational staff;
  - service acceptance procedures and criteria don't exist, or they do exist but are too demanding, too bureaucratic or not adhered to;
  - insufficient testing is conducted;
  - defects, incidents and problems identified during development and testing of new services and solutions are not identified or passed across to operational staff;

- there are no benefits realisation reviews or documentation of lessons learnt.

Technical support, operations and application management teams

The technical, operations and applications support and management teams are essential to problem managers and problem management activities. Their support and involvement in the analysis and resolution of problems is critical. In many organisations they are the principal resolver groups for many of the incidents and problems that arise. Without their involvement the problem manager's task would be almost impossible. It is essential that problem management and these resolver groups regularly collaborate in the following areas to ensure the effective and efficient resolution of incidents and problems continues.

- **Methods and techniques** – Problem managers need the support teams to assist them and support the use of the preferred problem management methods, techniques and processes.

- **Problem resolution** – Assistance with the resolution of incidents and problems.

- **Known errors** – Assistance with the identification and documentation of known errors and workarounds.

- **Knowledge sharing** – Involvement in the sharing of knowledge and the creation of knowledge articles.

- **Support information** – Maintenance of technical documentation and processes, and the production of technical guides and diagnostic scripts.

4 TOOLS, METHODS AND TECHNIQUES

This chapter describes the tools, methods and techniques used in the management and resolution of problems. These are many and varied, and many are referred to within service management industry standards and frameworks. The important service management industry standards and frameworks considered within this chapter are:

- the international standard on IT service management ISO/EC 20000 series;
- the ITIL framework;
- the COBIT® framework.

However, before considering these standards and frameworks, the following sections describe some of the frequently used generic problem management methods and techniques.

Typical tools and techniques used within the problem management process are:

- problem management and analysis techniques and tools used for the recording and management of all problems within an IT organisation;
- incident management and analysis techniques, and service desk tools, used for the recording and management of all incidents;
- the configuration management database (CMDB) for the management of IT assets and components through their lifecycles, including their relationships to other IT components;

- knowledge management tools and the SKMS for learning from past experience;
- the known error database (KEDB) for logging and referencing workarounds and quick fixes;
- statistical analysis and trending tools, such as spreadsheets;
- component failure impact analysis (CFIA) techniques;
- system failure analysis (SFA) techniques;
- risk identification, assessment and management.

IMPLEMENTATION, IMPROVEMENT TECHNIQUES AND PRACTICES

In many organisations problem management is one of the less developed service management processes. It seems that it is difficult for many organisations to establish problem management practices and activities successfully, yet problem management is one of the most powerful service management processes and has the potential to deliver significant benefit and value to the organisation. Some of the key challenges that organisations face in implementing problem management are:

- confusion (or a lack of differentiation between an incident and a problem);
- lack of skill, knowledge and capability around problem analysis, resolution and management;
- uncertainty about where and how to start tackling problem management;
- the inability to justify the benefit and value of investing in problem management;
- difficulties selecting the appropriate methods and techniques to analyse and resolve problems;
- focusing on the process rather than the purpose of the process (i.e. the management and resolution of the actual problems themselves);

- maintaining an appropriate balance between the resolution of incidents and the resolution of the underlying cause of incidents and problems.

Time should be spent understanding problem management practices and techniques and their benefits. Also, when starting out on the implementation of problem management, it is important that people with the right skills and attributes are selected as problem managers. They will be seen as the champions and role models for the process. It is vital that care is taken in the selection of personnel to lead the implementation of problem management practices within an organisation. More information on this aspect is included in Chapter 5.

Implementation practices

This section describes a suggested sequence for the implementation of problem management as a series of steps. The recommended sequence of ten steps is shown in Table 4.1, with each step described below.

Step 1: Agree the purpose, objectives and scope of problem management

The starting point for the implementation of any process is to define its purpose. The purpose of the problem management process, as defined earlier, is to:

- coordinate, lead, manage and continually improve problem management capability and activities within an organisation.

The main objectives of the role are to:

- minimise the business disruption caused by incidents and problems on an organisation;
- eliminate recurring incidents and the prevention of incidents and problems, through root cause analysis and the resolution of problems, wherever it is cost-effective to do so;

Table 4.1 The steps for implementing problem management

Step number	Step description
1	Agree the purpose, objectives and scope of problem management
2	Secure appropriate senior management commitment
3	Select a problem manager (a leader for problem management)
4	Talk to the business and customers
5	Baseline (where are we now?)
6	Identify and deliver 'quick wins'
7	Design and implement a simple and effective process (where do we want to be?)
8	Review the benefits and value (did we get there?)
9	Institutionalise the change
10	Move to continual improvement

- continually improve on the problem manager role and the problem management capability within the organisation.

Once the purpose and objectives have been agreed, then the scope of the problem management process and activities need to be defined and agreed. Initially, the scope of problem management may be defined and agreed to be quite small. However, as the capability of the people and the process increases, so should the scope be increased.

As mentioned before, the implementation of an effective problem management process is totally dependent upon the implementation and operation of an effective incident management process. The information recorded by incident management in incident records provides a starting point for a basic problem management process. If there is no incident management process, or it is ineffective, then it will be very difficult, if not impossible, to implement effective problem management.

However, the implementation of effective incident management is outside the scope of this book. Assuming therefore that effective incident management practices are in place, the next step is to gain commitment from senior management.

Step 2: Secure appropriate senior management commitment

It is important to have support from senior management, because the implementation of effective problem management will require time, money and resources. It will require separate resources from those used for incident management because the focus and objectives of the activities and the roles are different and often conflict. The skills, knowledge and attributes of a problem manager are different from those required by an incident manager. These aspects are considered in detail in Chapter 5.

Securing appropriate senior management commitment will normally require some form of business case. This will necessitate determining the benefit derived from the implementation of the selected problem management activities versus the costs involved, which means estimating the business benefits, impact and costs associated with the current incidents and problems. This information can then be compared with the estimated levels of benefits, impact and costs and the anticipated savings from effective problem management. This should involve obtaining feedback from stakeholders, customers and users on their challenges and perceptions. This will hopefully provide credibility, momentum and justification for further investment in the implementation of problem management activities. Some of the key benefits of problem management should be:

- reduction of service outage and business disruption through reductions in the volume of failure events, incidents and problems;

- improved incident resolution times through better incident matching, known errors and workarounds;

- reduction in customer and user complaints, frustration and 'pain';

- increases in effectiveness through reductions in failures, duplication and waste;

- reductions in the risk and impact of potential failures through the use of proactive problem techniques.

It is important to recognise at this early point in the implementation of problem management that this activity is not just the implementation of a process; like service management in general, it is much wider than that. This is part of a transformational or cultural change and needs to be planned accordingly. A good approach to be adopted is the eight-stage process, described in John P. Kotter's book *Leading Change*.[7]

1. **Establishing a sense of urgency** – Ensuring that there is sufficient drive and commitment to deliver the change.

2. **Creating a guiding coalition** – Assembling a group with enough power to lead the change.

3. **Developing a vision and strategy** – Developing a vision for the change and a strategy to achieve the vision.

4. **Communicating the change vision** – Ensuring that the vision is regularly reinforced and that there are the right role models for the expected behaviour.

5. **Empowering broad-based action** – Removing structures and obstacles that could block the change and empower action.

[7] Kotter, J.P. (1996) Leading change. Harvard Business School Press.

6. **Generating short-term wins** – Planning for and creating real performance improvements and wins, rewarding those that make the wins possible.

7. **Consolidating gains and producing more change** – Encourage change of areas that don't fit with the vision, developing people that can implement the change vision.

8. **Anchoring new approaches in the culture** – Create improved performance through customer and service focused behaviour, emphasising the connection between new behaviours and organisational success.

The implementation project to establish a basic problem management process should include all of these eight steps. Subsequent improvements should be completed using the CSI techniques discussed later.

Step 3: Select a problem manager (a leader for problem management)

The next step is to select a problem manager to lead the initiative. The selection of this person is critical to the success of the implementation of problem management. It needs to be someone who is a recognised achiever and is respected within the organisation. Often organisations select technical people for this role. This is not necessary and can often be counterproductive. While some understanding of technology and technical issues is required, it is actually more important for the problem manager to have a good knowledge of the business and its customers.

Step 4: Talk to the business and customers

A problem manager needs to understand:

- what the business of the organisation is;
- who the customers and users of IT services (both internal and external) are;
- which services they use;
- which business processes the services underpin;

- which critical business areas or vital business functions (VBFs) are supported;
- which IT services underpin the VBFs and are therefore critical;
- what business impact/disruption is caused when services are unavailable.

This information can only be obtained from stakeholders, customers and users, unless there is an accurate and up-to-date service catalogue containing this information. Yet even then, it is still important that the problem manager talks to the business and customers and understands their areas of 'pain' and 'frustration'. This will provide valuable information on what will be the important initial areas for problem management to focus on.

Step 5: Baseline (where are we now?)

Take some baseline figures on the amount of 'pain', disruption, cost and frustration caused by incidents and problems. This activity should try to measure the current level of service as perceived by the stakeholders, customers and users of the services. This can then be used as a baseline for comparison during the implementation of the problem management process and will enable the degree of improvement made in the level of service to be measured. Make sure that measurements (key performance indicators (KPIs)/metrics) are in place before and after the process changes have been implemented. Based on the results of this baseline outcome(s), objectives and measurable targets should be set for the problem management implementation to deliver, so that the success of the implementation can be assessed.

One of the frameworks or standards, for example ITIL or ISO/ IEC 20000, could be used as the basis for the conducting the baseline review.

Step 6: Identify and deliver 'quick wins'

The temptation when starting as a problem manager is to create many problem records. However, initially it is better to identify and focus on a few key problem records based on the results of a 'pain value' analysis (see page 93) or Pareto analysis (see page 118). This will help to focus attention and resources on a few critical areas and deliver some early wins. It can often take a long time to implement a mature problem management process, so it is important that benefits can be demonstrated early to stakeholders and senior management to secure their ongoing interest, support and commitment. Common 'quick wins' for problem management are:

- resolving commonly recurring incidents;

- identifying known errors and workarounds for the 'top ten incidents' from a business disruption perspective;

- reducing the impact of major incidents and service outages to critical services;

- addressing major areas of customer and user dissatisfaction and complaint;

- addressing services, technology or components with high volumes of incidents or high rates of failure – these are often the main areas of service failure and customer dissatisfaction.

These initial 'quick wins' can then be used to justify and secure more investment and resources.

EXAMPLE – QUICK WIN

The IT service desk of a major international organisation was handling approximately 4,000 incidents per week. The number of service desk agents was reduced in December to save costs. However, in the following five months (January to May), it started to struggle with the volume of incidents. The service desk manager had requested additional resources for the service desk, but this request had been rejected. The service desk manager then printed the number of incidents opened and closed each month and although there had been an issue with the number of closed incidents in January and February, it looked as though the situation was improving.

A problem manager was asked to assist the service desk manager to see what could be done to improve the situation. The problem manager decided to examine not just the number of incidents being opened and closed each month, but also the associated incident backlog. The graph in Figure 4.1 was produced.

Figure 4.1 Graph 1 for an example 'quick win'

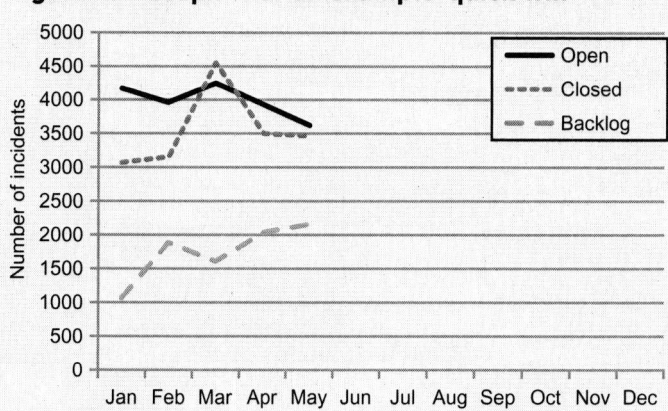

This highlighted the issue of the incident backlog doubling within that five-month period. The problem manager and service manager decided to take action. A brainstorming session, conducted by the problem manager, was convened with representatives from all areas involved in incident management. It was decided that an improvement plan should be instigated. The main improvement actions agreed to were:

- identify the 'top ten' incidents each week and make the workarounds/resolutions known to everyone;

- concentrate problem management resources on resolving the 'top ten' incidents each week;

- publicise workarounds and known errors making them easier and more and visible for the service desk;

- improve incident matching techniques;
- encourage all areas to share knowledge and information on incident resolution;
- encourage all areas, including the service desk, to resolve and close as many incidents as possible.

These six improvements were introduced during June and July and had little immediate effect, but as they became more familiar and more widely used, more incidents were closed and the backlog reduced significantly as shown in Figure 4.2.

Figure 4.2 Graph 2 for an example 'quick win'

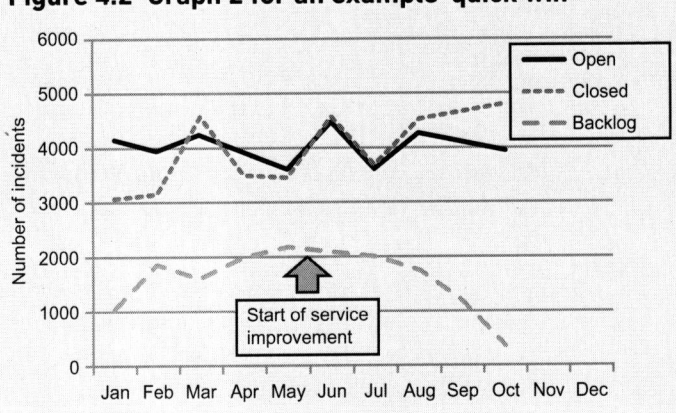

The quality of service to the users was improved and the overall business disruption caused by IT services was significantly reduced.

Step 7: Design and implement a simple and effective process (where do we want to be?)

This step is all about designing and implementing a simple, pragmatic and effective problem management process. In many organisations some problem management practices will already exist. Don't throw these away and just implement a theoretical problem management process based on ITIL, ISO/IEC 20000 or COBIT®. Review the existing practices and build on the good aspects of them and reduce or remove any bad elements.

Within many organisations there will be some reactive problem management activities already being performed. Generally these are very much focused on specific internal and technical issues within individual support teams or resolver groups. The practices therefore are generally inconsistent and incompatible, resulting in little coordination and consistency and causing major issues when problems span a team, group or technology boundary. However, wherever possible, use and build on existing processes and practices because this will facilitate the buy-in and take up of new processes.

Another issue that is likely to arise is that of the 'hero culture'. Some support teams or resolver groups like solving incidents. Team leaders and managers reward and encourage the behaviour of the 'technical expert' who enjoys being the hero and solving technical incidents time and time again. This often means that they aren't interested in solving the underlying cause of incidents, because the more incidents they solve the bigger their reputation grows as the 'technical expert'. They are reluctant to share their knowledge and expertise and to resolve problems because this would actually reduce their importance and status within the organisation. This is why the involvement of all support and resolver groups in the early development of problem management practices is so vital to their ultimate success.

These are just some of the cultural issues that problem managers have to address when trying to introduce common problem techniques and practices within an organisation. It is important that these cultural issues are addressed early if 'quick wins' are going to be delivered. Some brainstorming sessions, which include representatives from all teams, could be helpful here and could be used to:

- identify good practices to build on;
- identify bad or broken practices to remove or reduce their use;
- break barriers between teams;
- build relationships and establish 'team working' practices and collaborative effort;
- listen to customers and areas of 'pain' and frustration;
- establish a 'virtual problem management team' with representatives and involvement from all key areas, especially the resolver groups;
- identify a 'road map', schedule, milestones, outcomes and success criteria for problem management;
- identify risks, constraints and barriers.

Remember that standards and frameworks are guidelines and should not be implemented verbatim. Rather, they should be adopted, examined and then adapted to fit the specific requirements of the organisation. The most common causes of failure of problem management processes are complex, theoretical or bureaucratic processes that deliver little benefit or value to the business, customers and users. Focus should be on the implementation of simple, effective processes that work.

If there are no existing problem management practices in place, then concentrate on the basic areas of problem management first:

- Reactive problem management activities.
- Identification of known errors and workarounds.
- Problem management education and training, ensuring that people understand the significance and differences between incidents and problems, and their resolution.

These basic areas are probably the simplest and easiest to implement, and can help to deliver the 'quick wins', mentioned earlier. Even if some problem management activities exist within an organisation, these are good areas to address first. Once established, they can provide a solid base for subsequently developing the more complex proactive problem management practices.

Good education and training is vital to the success of problem management within an organisation. This should cover:

- **for support team and resolver group leaders** – the importance of a consistent approach, the culture, the techniques, knowledge sharing and the benefits of problem management. They need to be the role models for their teams;

- **for all areas and people** – the importance of following problem management processes, the techniques and procedures, and knowledge sharing;

- **for senior management** – the importance of continually re-enforcing the message and acting as role models by using the techniques themselves when making management decisions. If senior management really grasp and use problem management policies and practices, then this will speed up the cultural change of the organisation.

Understand what is required initially from problem management, ensure that the initial outcomes are achieved and make it easier for people to do things the right way. This will mean that everyone will want to work with you and you will maintain the interest and commitment of senior management and the customers.

Select a set of problem management methods and techniques that is appropriate for the organisation. Don't try and use all of them. Involve all areas, particularly the resolver groups, in the selection of these to ensure that all requirements are considered and that the most relevant techniques are used for all areas. Establish the problem management team as the 'centre of excellence' for the techniques and ensure that appropriate information, education and training is provided for all areas. Encourage the selected techniques and workarounds to become the way of doing things in all areas. These need to be reviewed and revised regularly to ensure:

- their continued acceptability, effectiveness and suitability;
- reduce business disruption;
- they are visible and easily accessible by service desk and incident management staff.

A dedicated problem management resource or team should be established, separate from the service desk and incident management resources. The size of the resource required will depend upon the amount of support and involvement obtained from support teams and resolver groups.

Once the basic reactive aspects of problem management are accepted and well used, the proactive aspects of the problem management process can be developed and implemented and the problem process can be integrated with other process areas.

The process, methods and techniques should always be selected and designed first. The tool(s) to be used to automate the problem management process and practices should then be considered and selected subsequently. This ensures that the right process is implemented for the organisation rather than a process that suits the tool(s) – even if the process might subsequently need to be 'tweaked' or adjusted to fit the requirements of the tool(s) as a compromise. The alternative is often a lot of time and resource spent in customising and tailoring the tool(s) to meet the specific, additional requirements of the process (which is not an effective use of problem management time and resources).

The final aspects of the process to consider are the measurements, metrics and reporting. These aspects are covered more fully in 'The problem lifecycle' on page 132 and 'Problem categorisation' on page 134. The implemented process and the supporting tool(s) need to be capable of providing the correct information for the next step – the review of the benefits and value of problem management. It is essential therefore that the process is capable of delivering the measurements and reports required to demonstrate the outcome(s) of the activities.

Step 8: Review the benefits and value (did we get there?)

Step 8 ensures that, after a suitable period of time, problem management practices are reviewed for success. A benefits realisation review should compare the actual achievements from the implementation against the predicted outcome(s), the objectives, the benefits and the agreed success criteria, metrics and targets.

As a part of this benefits realisation review a new baseline should be taken. The results and measurements (metrics and KPIs) from this baseline should be compared with those contained within the previous baseline (step 5). This will give a good indication about what progress has been made since the initial baseline.

Either the implementation will have realised all of its outcomes, objectives, benefits and targets, or there will have been some deviations from them. The reason for any deviations should be understood. The deviations should be investigated and perhaps some remedial actions implemented or some further improvements should be instigated for the future.

Finally the results and measurements, metrics and KPIs should be reviewed to see whether they are still relevant and applicable. If they are not, then they should be revised and a new set agreed. A new baseline should be taken and a new set of targets agreed, based on the new measurements, metrics and KPIs. This can then be used as a basis for measuring further improvements.

Step 9: Institutionalise the change

This step should ensure that a process owner and a process manger are appointed for the problem management process. These roles are explained in greater detail in Chapter 3. Often these roles are assigned to a problem manager to ensure the ongoing success of the problem management practices is maintained.

The other actions that need to be taken now are:

- consolidating problem management activities and responsibilities into everyone's everyday role or job description – this will ensure consistent involvement in the process and reduce the need for extensive dedicated problem management resources;
- continually emphasising the need for:
  - focusing on the reduction of business disruption and pain;
  - focusing on the increase of customer and user satisfaction.
  - measuring and publicising the success of problem management;
  - reinforcing the messages around the continued use of and conformance to the problem management policies and process.

These actions will help to facilitate the cultural change. They will ensure that problem management is embedded within the culture of the organisation and becomes the standard way of thinking and acting.

Step 10: Move to continual improvement

Once a simple and effective problem management process has been established, it needs to include ongoing review and improvement. If there is already a CSI culture and process then problem management should work closely with CSI, as described on page 77.

If there is no CSI process, the problem manager should continually review and improve problem management practices, rapidly developing a proactive capability. Problem management should then use this activity to drive the need to establish a CSI culture and process. Again this should be achieved with the support and commitment of senior management and key stakeholders. This can be started by establishing a CSI register, and encouraging and collecting ideas and suggestions for improvement from all areas. However, if this is done, it is essential that some of the improvement suggestions are prioritised, approved and implemented. If not, the initiative will lose focus and credibility and the processes will become ineffective.

Improvement practices

No matter how mature and capable problem management practices are, they can always be improved. Therefore, problem management should work closely with CSI to ensure that improvements continue to reduce the disruption caused by incidents and problems, both reactively and proactively.

Once a CSI culture and CSI process are established within the organisation, implementation is replaced by continual review and improvement. Care must be taken to ensure that improvements are always driven by enhancing the outcome of the process from a business, customer and user perspective. Sometimes improvement suggestions can be submitted based on improving the process itself. If an improvement does not make something better, faster or cheaper for the business, the customer or the user, then it should be replaced by one that does.

PROBLEM ANALYSIS METHODS AND TECHNIQUES

This section contains an explanation of the many and varied methods and techniques used for the management and resolution of problems. There is overlap between the various methods, and each organisation should 'adopt and adapt' the method(s) best suited to their needs and operation. Most of the problem methods and techniques can be used with a variety of problem types and circumstances. In the initial stages of problem management it is worth focusing on a few key problem techniques and getting familiar with them before trying to master additional techniques.

Most problem management methods and techniques are heavily dependent on a good incident management process that accurately maintains a comprehensive set of up-to-date incident records.

Use of known errors, workarounds and knowledge articles

The purpose of using known errors, workarounds and knowledge articles is to:

- be able to match new events and incidents to events and incidents that have happened before so that they can be quickly and effectively managed and resolved;
- minimise the business disruption caused by incidents and problems;
- learn from past experience and not 'reinvent the wheel'.

The creation of known errors, workarounds and knowledge articles helps organisations resolve incidents and problems faster, which means that the business disruption experienced as a result of an error or failure within the services can be greatly reduced. Therefore one of the most important approaches to the management and resolution of problems is to determine the root cause and establish workarounds for each problem. This is particularly vital for high impact incidents or problems or complex problems that are going to take time to analyse and resolve. Once a root cause and workaround have been determined, a known error record can be created, either containing or referencing details of the workaround. This known error record needs to be linked to all relevant incident and problem records so that other incidents that occur can be matched to the known error record and the workaround can be quickly applied. In some cases the workaround can be scripted and automatically applied without manual intervention, thereby reducing disruption and saving time.

However, the underlying root cause of the problem still needs to be analysed and a permanent resolution developed and applied in order to remove the source of further incidents and problems. If the problem is a really complex problem, a number of increasingly effective workarounds might be developed and applied in order to reduce the business impact of the problem. This situation is illustrated in the three scenarios shown in Figures 4.3–4.5.

Scenario 1 (in Figure 4.3) shows the impact of an incident occurring that has no workaround. It is a complex incident and it takes a long time to analyse the root cause and resolve the underlying problem. Therefore the business disruption caused is considerable as is indicated by the shaded area.

Figure 4.3 Problem scenario 1

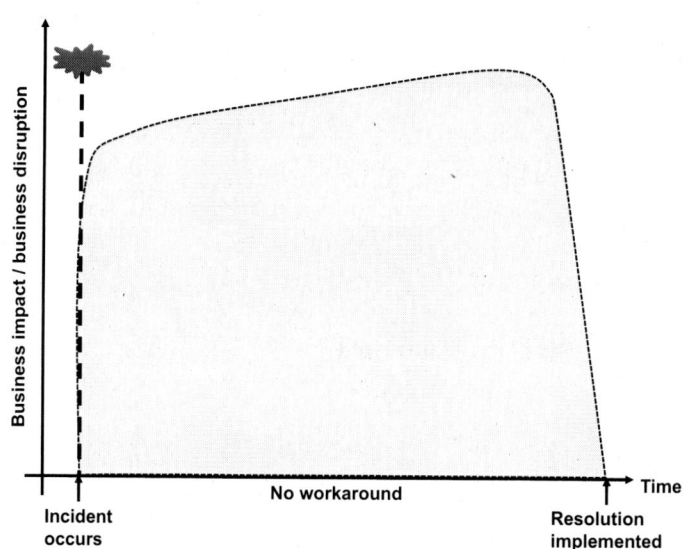

Scenario 2 (in Figure 4.4) shows the same situation, but in this scenario time is spent on identifying the root cause and then developing and applying a workaround, before resolving the root cause of the underlying problem. The overall resolution time is the same yet the business disruption caused is greatly reduced as indicated by the darker shaded area. The impact of the incident and problem on the business therefore has been greatly reduced by implementing the workaround.

Figure 4.4 Problem scenario 2

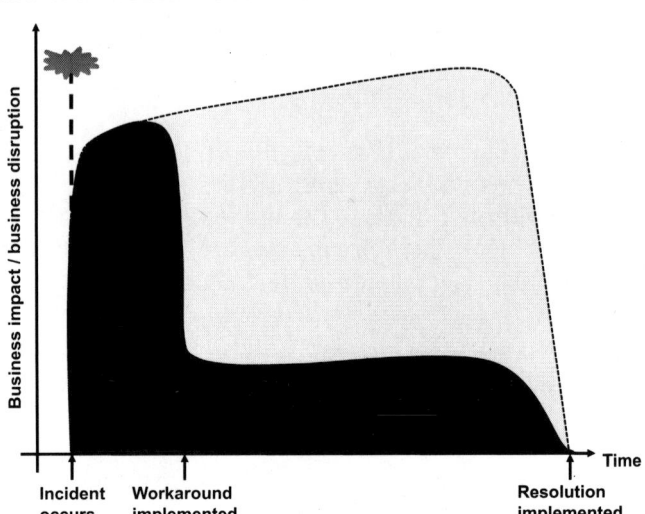

Figure 4.5 Problem scenario 3

In scenario 3 (in Figure 4.5), time has been spent analysing and developing a second workaround that completely removes the business disruption of the incident – again indicated by

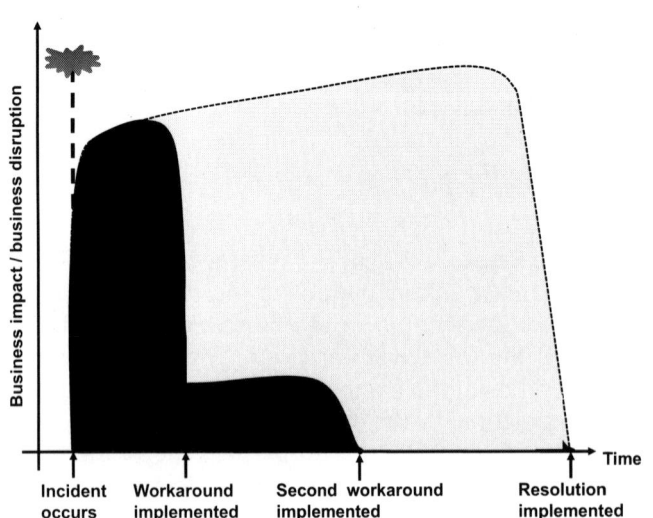

the darker shaded area. In this case, not only is the business disruption reduced still further, but the time taken to analyse and resolve the underlying root cause of the problem can take a longer elapsed time, with no additional impact on the business.

These three scenarios illustrate the power and importance of developing and applying workarounds to minimise the business disruption caused by incidents and problems.

When a workaround is developed and successfully applied to a situation, it is important that the problem record remains open and that all incidents, known errors and workarounds are linked to the problem record. It is also vital that the status and content of all relevant records are accurately updated and maintained in a timely fashion.

EXAMPLE – WORKAROUND

An internal IT service provider operates a major multitier website for its organisation. The website processes millions of transactions every day. The web server farm provides the home pages and much of the content. It consists of a number of 'load balanced' web servers and is spread across the two data centres. The original web servers were running out of capacity and were replaced by newer, faster web servers, resulting in eight new web servers in each data centre.

These new web servers initially provide much faster response than the previous web servers. However, after a period of time they start to experience issues with the web server software, responding very slowly to page requests. This disrupts the website, giving inconsistent response to website visitors. A problem record is created and all the incidents are linked to the problem record. A workaround is associated with the problem ensuring that each subsequent incident is then quickly resolved by reloading the affected server.

The issue is reported to the webstore software supplier, but a solution is not forthcoming. On each occurrence another incident is raised, linked to the problem and known error, and the affected web server is manually reloaded and returned to service. The business managers responsible for the website are demanding a solution to the issue.

The supplier is chased for a solution and pressure is put on them to resolve the issue, but still nothing is forthcoming. Meanwhile the problem manager organises a problem review meeting, with representatives from all of the relevant technical support teams, to look into the possibility of developing an improved workaround. After some discussion the server support people agree to develop a script with the help of the network support team that:

- periodically tests the response time of each of the web servers; and
- if the response from any of the web servers is 'slow':
  - removes the web server from the web server farm;
  - reloads the web server;
  - checks the response of the reloaded web server;
  - returns the web server to the web server farm.

This first workaround, also recorded within the known error, proves quite successful and satisfies the business managers for a while because the impact on visitors to the website is greatly reduced. However, despite increased pressure on the supplier they still have not provided a solution to the issue. The business managers are again getting increasingly agitated about the continued disruption to the website, especially during periods of high volume web traffic.

The problem manager again reviews the problem, talks to the business managers and realises that the current workaround is no longer acceptable. Another problem review meeting is held to investigate what other options are available. During the discussions on the scope and definition of the problem it is realised that the 'slow response' only started to occur when servers have been running for several days, so the server support team are asked to develop a new script that will reload each of the web servers, in sequence, at 2:00 a.m. each morning because this is the period of lowest web traffic. This information is recorded within the associated known error. This second workaround removes the website disruption completely and the business managers are satisfied that as far as they are concerned the problem has been resolved. There is no further disruption to the website.

Although no further incidents are raised, the problem record is kept open and the pressure is still put on the supplier to solve the issue. Some months later the supplier eventually provides a new release of the web server software that completely solves the issue. After testing, the web server software is upgraded on each of the web servers in the web farm. However, because the second workaround has been so successful and no failures had occurred since it had been implemented, it is retained even after the upgraded software was installed.

Creative problem solving

Alex Osborn and Dr Sydney Parne started developing creative problem solving methods in 1939 and trademarked the name Creative Problem Solving™ (CPS). They were the first to develop and use brainstorming (see page 100) and other CPS techniques. The structured CPS method was initially developed as a seven-step process that evolved subsequently through a number of refinements and improvements to its current CPS framework, consisting of the following steps contained in four areas (as shown in Figure 4.6).

Figure 4.6 The creative problem solving (CPS) framework

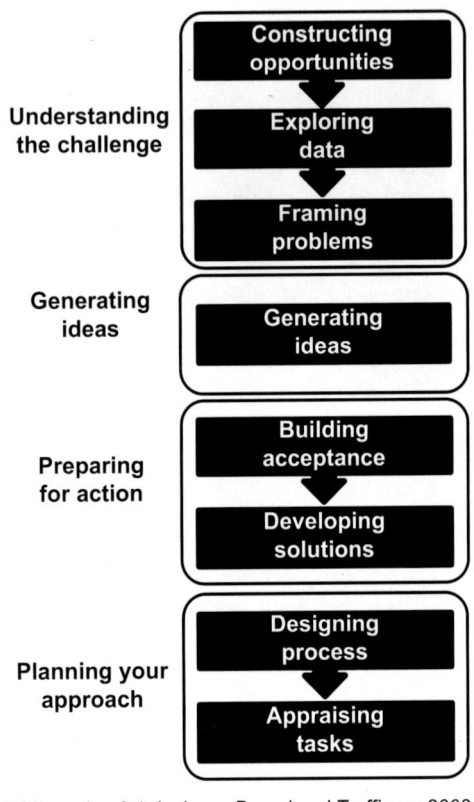

Based on CPS version 6.1: Isaksen, Dorval and Treffinger 2003

CPS techniques provide a structured approach to the solving of problems, which encourages the use of novel and innovative approaches and solutions. A solution is considered creative if components that are readily available can be used, and when there is a short time limit within which to solve the problem. These techniques are designed to reframe the problem or to shift a person's mental approach into one that encourages creativity. The following is a brief description of the four areas of CPS:

- **Understanding the challenge** – This consists of three steps and involves exploring a broad issue or challenge that needs to be resolved. It includes collecting, assembling and analysing information about the issue and then identifying, agreeing and defining the main issue and the focus of attention.

- **Constructing opportunities** – This first step details and considers the main challenges and explores the associated opportunities by identifying the main targets and goals.

- **Exploring data** – Collects and analyses the data and information from many different areas.

- **Framing problems** – Subsequently looks at different ways of describing the challenge(s) and endeavours to describe them in a way that motivates everyone towards achieving the main agreed targets and goals.

- **Generating ideas** – There is only one step in this section, which is focused on brainstorming and capturing as many new ideas and suggestions as possible. This is usually achieved by assembling a group or groups of people and should encourage lateral thinking and any potential ideas or suggestions.

- **Preparing for action** – This section consists of two steps and involves discussing and exploring the ideas and suggestions, and developing potential approaches and opportunities into workable solutions.

  - **Building acceptance** – Develops support and consensus for the selected approach(es) and solution(s) and devises plans and checkpoints to review the effectiveness of the selected option(s).

  - **Developing solutions** – Applies policies and techniques to analyse, review and revise potential possibilities and refine them into probable solutions.

- **Planning the approach** – There are two steps contained within this section and they focus on monitoring what progress is being made and ensuring that progress is being made in the right direction.

  - **Designing process** – Ensures that the right CPS aspects, tools and techniques are used in the most appropriate way to realise objectives.

- **Appraising tasks** – Appraises the CPS overall approach and ensures that the right method, tasks and resources are being used effectively in the resolution of the issue.

Many of the concepts and techniques involved and initiated within CPS have been developed and incorporated into many other problem management methods.[8]

Root cause analysis

Root cause analysis (RCA) is a problem solving method that tries to identify and solve the root cause of recorded incidents and problems, rather than just repeatedly treating the symptoms of incidents. By focusing on the resolution of the root cause, then recurrence of the incidents and the problems can be prevented. It is probably the most important of all of the problem management techniques, and it is definitely a key skill required by all problem managers. The use of this technique is not restricted to IT service provision – it can also be applied in many other industries for analysing, resolving and preventing potential failures and accidents.

RCA can be an expensive and time-consuming activity. Before attempting RCA of a problem, the following activities should be completed to ensure that RCA is focused on the relevant problems and areas:

1. Before commencing RCA, the problem should be analysed, clearly defined and documented using one or more problem analysis techniques, such as:

    - the five whys (see page 103);
    - chronological analysis (see page 90);
    - Ishikawa diagrams (see page 112);
    - brainstorming (see page 100).

---

[8] More information on the CPS framework, activities, techniques and tools can be found in Isaksen, S.G., Dorval, K.B. and Treffinger, D.J. (2010) Creative Approaches To Problem Solving – A Framework For Innovation and Change.

2. The business impact and the priority of open problem records should be regularly reviewed so all problems can be prioritised. This will ensure that RCA is being performed on those problems that are having the biggest impact on the business first. This would involve using one or more problem analysis techniques, such as:

   • pain value analysis (see page 93);

   • Pareto analysis (see page 118).

3. If it is anticipated that RCA and resolution of the problem could take a long time, attempts should be made to devise and implement cost-effective workarounds that decrease the business impact of the problem, before attempting resolution of the problem itself (as described on page 78).

4. These actions might need to be repeated a number of times before starting on RCA of a problem, because workarounds will change the business impact of the problem.

   This is important because it is often better to identify and implement a workaround to a problem than it is to perform RCA and correct or resolve the problem. This is particularly true when it is possible that an effective workaround can be quickly designed and implemented, whereas full RCA might be a potentially long and expensive process. Also, this enables problem resources to be redirected and focused on alternative high priority problems that have no effective workaround.

It is possible that a problem might have more than one root cause and therefore several resolutions or corrective actions might need to be implemented. RCA can therefore be an iterative method. Without understanding the root cause, it is impossible to determine an effective resolution of a problem – the one leads to the other.

The sequence of RCA activities should be:

1. Define the problem by identifying the factors, sequence, timing, scope and impact of events and actions that caused the failure or issue. Comprehensive and accurate problem definition descriptions and event sequences are critical to successful problem resolution. Describe all of the symptoms of the problem and all of the undesirable outcomes. This should include identification of variances from procedures or normal operations.

2. A logical structured approach should be adopted during the RCA using a thorough analysis of all of the available evidence. Ask 'why' each of the events happened and 'why' each action was taken, within the documented timeline, and validate the effects they had.

3. All possible causes should be considered and the most plausible causes and their resolutions agreed. This normally involves a team of people from different areas of the organisation. Conclusions, recommendations and corrective actions should be documented and agreed for resolution for each of the causes. Validate that if each corrective action was implemented before the event, then the harmful impact would have been reduced or completely removed.

4. There might be more than one root cause of a problem, so timelines of events and actions need to be explained and the relationship between events, factors, impacts and causes understood. This is so that each of the causes of the problem can be eliminated and prevented from occurring again in the future, or at least their impact reduced.

5. Alternative courses of action will need to be identified and investigated with agreed outcomes defined for each planned resolution of the problem. The most cost-effective solutions can then be selected for implementation.

6. Agree within the group the course(s) of action to be taken and the schedule for completing it, with defined review and revision points. All actions

should be owned with agreed timescales for their completion.

7. Once agreed, validate and confirm the course(s) of action, agreeing within the group that:

   • with a reasonable degree of certainty, that if the course(s) of action had been implemented before the documented events, it would have prevented their occurrence or at least prevented or reduced their impact;

   • the course(s) of action will have no other undesirable effects or impacts, or at least, if it does they are within acceptable limits.

8. Implement the agreed course(s) of action, completing the planned reviews and adjusting any courses of action, where necessary with those concerned. If any other undesirable effects or events are experienced ensure that they are appropriately recorded and managed. If major issues occur with the agreed course(s) of action, then the exercise might need to be repeated, with a revised definition of the problem (step 1).

9. Subsequent to the successful implementation of the resolution of the problem and an appropriate delay, an independent review of the problem should be performed. This should be completed by someone familiar with problem management objectives and procedures, but not involved with this particular problem resolution. The objective of this review should be:

   • to review and quantify the success of the resolution;

   • to establish:

     ▪ what we did that was right;
     ▪ what we did that was wrong;
     ▪ what lessons we learnt;
     ▪ how we can do it better next time;

- how we can improve RCA and problem management procedures;
- to update the service knowledge management system (SKMS) appropriately with lessons learnt and any other relevant knowledge articles.

All of these activities should be completed without attributing blame. The objective should always be focused on implementing successful problem resolutions and improving problem management knowledge, procedures and capability.

RCA is principally used reactively to resolve events and failures once they have occurred, but it can also be used proactively to prevent potential events and failures from happening in the future. The technique can be used to examine and understand potential scenario events and failures, determine the root cause and implement preventative action, before they actually occur. Used effectively in this manner it can transform the culture of an organisation, from an organisation that spends its time and resources continually reacting to failures and crises to one that proactively reduces the frequency and impact of incidents and problems. This will require support from other areas within the organisation, particularly senior management because there may be resistance to this approach from other groups and teams.

Chronological analysis

Chronological analysis is often used in the analysis of complex incidents and problems, in particular when there are conflicting reports about what has happened and when. This technique is very useful when analysing complex problems because it helps to break the problem down into many smaller steps. Each of the smaller steps can then be analysed separately. It involves investigating, analysing, collating and recording the sequence and timing of events leading up to a problem or an incident. Often the times have to be 'normalised' to account for different timings or time zones between different components and systems to get a 'real time' picture of events.

This technique can also be useful when investigating intermittent or infrequently occurring failures or when comparing sequences of events within a set of associated incidents. It allows the similarities as well as the differences between the timings of each occurrence to be identified. The sequence or chain of events between the cause and effect of incidents and problems can then be determined, evaluated and documented. This method can be used to identify the root cause of a set of incidents or a problem and ultimately lead to their resolution. This technique is often used to develop the problem definition, in conjunction with other problem analysis and management methods and techniques.

EXAMPLE – CHRONOLOGICAL ANALYSIS

An internal IT provider organisation has an incident management process and a well-established service desk. There is no problem manager or problem management process. The service desk is recording over 2,000 incidents a week, many of which are chase requests for progress updates to previously raised incident records. Often the service desk analysts can find no record of any incident record being raised. There are also comments and complaints from users that the response from the service desk is inconsistent. However, initial reports and analysis of incident volumes and responses show that over 90 per cent of incidents are being resolved within their agreed SLA targets.

The service desk manager decides, with support from her manager, to start investigating the situation. She creates a problem description:

Inconsistent progress and resolution response rate to incidents by the service desk

She then analyses some of the incident records in a bit more detail, rather than relying on the regular incident management reports. She talks to users, customers and service desk analysts and discovers that the principal area of concern is around incidents raised by emails from users. On more detailed analysis of individual emails, incidents and incident records, she finds there is a similar, chronological sequence of events (shown in Table 4.2).

Table 4.2 Chronological analysis example

Day	Time	Event
1	09:30	User creates email of incident and sends to the service desk email address
	09:31	Email received in service desk email inbox
2		Nothing
3		Nothing
4	10:30	User chases the incident. The service desk analyst response is that nothing has been received. User says they sent an email three days ago
	10:35	Service desk analyst creates an incident record dated and timed (Day 4 at 10:35, with the details provided by the user)
	10:40	Service desk analyst removes the email from the service desk inbox.
5	14:45	Incident resolved and incident record updated
	14:50	Incident resolution confirmed with the users and the incident record is closed

Further analysis of the emails received shows that many emails are left in the inbox for at least three or four days before a service desk incident is raised. Whenever incident records are raised they are given the date and time of when the incident record is created, rather than the date and time of the receipt of the email. In some cases emails had waited over a week before incident records were raised.

This explains the difference between the experience of the users and the statistics and reports produced by the service desk. As a result, the service desk manager implements a procedure for the service desk to review the service desk email account and create a new incident record for each email as it is received. Subsequently the service provided to the users is improved and the number of comments and complaints received by the service desk is greatly reduced. This procedure is subsequently automated with the service desk tool, which improves the service still further.

Pain value analysis

This method can be used in a situation where there are a number of concurrent problems that need to be analysed simultaneously. It is used to prioritise incidents and problems for analysis, rather than the actual analysis and resolution of them. It helps to evaluate the 'pain', business impact or business disruption caused by incidents and problems and enables problem managers to focus on those incidents and problems causing the greatest organisational 'pain' rather than less disruptive ones.

A simple formula can be used and agreed with the business to calculate the 'pain value' of a particular set of incidents and problems. This could be based on:

- the duration of the failures;
- the cost of failures to the business or the business disruption experienced;
- the loss of potential sales or the loss of productivity;
- the number of users impacted by the failures.

EXAMPLE – PAIN VALUE ANALYSIS

The graph in Figure 4.7 plots the number of outstanding problems for this month and the corresponding pain value within each of the problem categories.

Figure 4.7 An example of pain value analysis

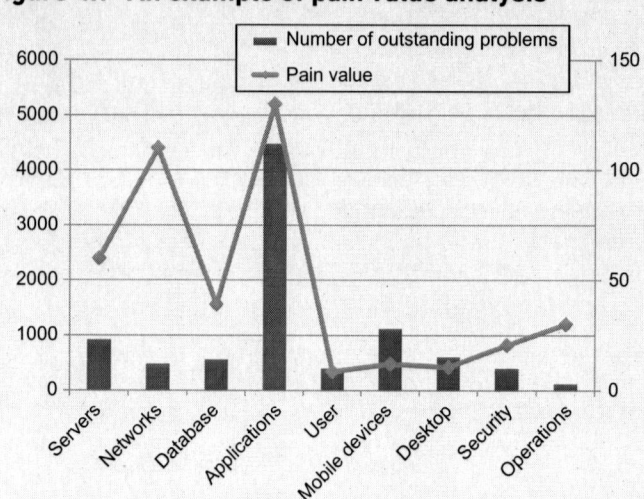

From this graph it can be seen that the problem categories with the greatest number of problems are:

- applications;
- mobile devices.

The problem categories with the biggest 'pain value', causing the greatest business disruption are:

- applications;
- networks.

So, although networks is the category with the fifth highest number of outstanding problems, it causes the second highest level of 'pain value' on the graph. This is second only to the level of business disruption caused by problems in the applications category. All of the other problem categories are causing much lower levels of pain. This would tend to indicate that the two key problem areas to focus on are those problems within the applications and networks categories. In fact the two categories with the highest 'pain value' per problem are networks and operations. So each problem solved within these categories would reduce the overall 'pain value' or business disruption by the largest amount.

Kepner–Tregoe method

The Kepner–Tregoe problem-solving method provides a formal approach and set of steps for analysing and resolving problems.[9] Solutions are recommended and implemented to remove or reduce the impact of the underlying root causes of problems. The method proves particularly useful when formality and structure is needed, for instance, when tackling complex problems, major problems or problems with a major business impact.

The Kepner–Tregoe approach describes a problem as the visible effect of a cause that resides somewhere in the past. The approach is based on four basic patterns of thinking:

- **Assessing and clarifying** – This is about trying to answer the question, 'What's going on?'

- **Relating cause to effect** – This is about relating an event, cause or issue to its outcome or effect.

- **Making choices** – This concerns making choices between alternative possible resolution approaches. It drives three main activities:

  - Definition of the purpose and outcomes.

---

[9] Kepner, C.H. and Tregoe, B.B. (2006) The New Rational Manager. Kepner-Tregoe Publishing.

- Consideration of available alternatives.
- Assessment of the relative likelihood and risks of the available alternatives.

- **Anticipating the future** – This is about imagining the future, that is, 'What could happen?' and 'What would be the good and the bad outcomes from the available alternative approaches?'

These four basic patterns give rise to the four basic rational processes of Kepner–Tregoe that follow.

Situation appraisal

Situation appraisal enables the best possible use to be made of the other three processes of Kepner–Tregoe. Often when an issue or situation occurs there is confusion and a mass of information, some relevant and some irrelevant. It is very difficult to sort out important information from insignificant and irrelevant information. Other problem analysis techniques are often used to assist with the definition and clarification of the issue or concern,[10] such as chronological analysis (see page 90) or the 'five whys?' (see page 103). A clear definition of the problem should be produced and actions identified, prioritised, instigated and monitored. The situation appraisal activities are shown in Figure 4.8.

This sequence of activities can be described briefly as:

1. Concerns should be identified, listed and documented.
2. All concerns should be reviewed and clarified. Some are complex and might need to be detailed and broken down into a number of simple concerns.
3. All concerns should be prioritised based on three factors:

   - The seriousness of the current business impact.
   - The urgency of the concern.
   - Any evidence that the seriousness will grow?

---

[10] A concern is defined as any situation that causes an individual to feel the need to act.

4. The high priority or critical concerns should be focused on and addressed first with the appropriate type and amount of analysis: problem analysis, decision analysis or potential problem and opportunity analysis.

5. Each concern then needs to be reviewed to determine:

   ▪ who needs to be involved;
   ▪ what needs to be done and when;
   ▪ who will do what;
   ▪ who will document the progress and results.

Figure 4.8 Kepner–Tregoe situation appraisal activities

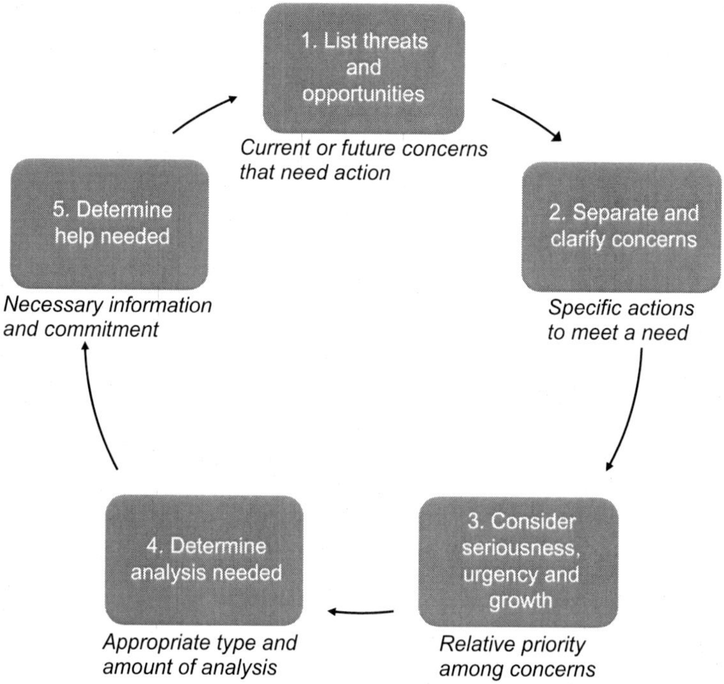

Based on situation appraisal techniques: Kepner–Tregoe 2006

Problem analysis

Problem analysis begins with the development of a problem statement and answering the question 'Why?' Resolution of the cause(s) of the problem is based on linking the effects of the problem back to its 'exact' cause(s). Problem analysis is used to describe and define a situation where for some reason the expected level of performance is not being achieved (the performance deviation) and the cause of the deviation is not yet known. Problem analysis requires a structured approach based around the use of a table/form.

The analysis continues by answering four questions:

- What?
- Where?
- When?
- Extent?

A table or spreadsheet should be created for each problem, so information on the answers can be recorded.

Decision analysis

The decision analysis stage of the process starts with the development of a 'decision statement' or by describing all of the alternative 'decision choices'. Decision analysis then consists of answering the following questions:

- To what purpose?
- Which?
- How?

Measurable objectives need to be developed for the decision-making procedure, together with a minimum set of requirements. Also the criteria to be used when making the decision should be defined and agreed. These criteria should be divided into 'MUSTS' (mandatory requirements) and 'WANTS' (non-mandatory requirements). The best alternative or the most appropriate alternative should then be selected and this is the alternative that fulfils all of the 'MUSTS' and most of the 'WANTS', most comprehensively. Often some 'WANTS' are more significant and should therefore be given a higher weighting within the decision-making procedure.

The final stage of decision analysis is to assess all of the adverse consequences of each potential alternative course of action. This involves listing each adverse consequence in terms of the:

- likelihood or probability of it occurring (e.g. high, medium or low);

- the seriousness or size of the impact (e.g. high, medium or low).

Potential problem and opportunity analysis

Potential problem and opportunity analysis consists of looking into the future at the possible threats and opportunities associated with each course of action. The results of this activity are then used to take the most appropriate action now. Potential problem and opportunity analysis enables us to change the future by influencing the decisions and the courses of action taken now. Considering the future consequences of each course of action ensures that the option that has the best possible future outcome is selected. Problem analysis and decision analysis are driven by current events, whereas potential problem and opportunity analysis proactively considers the future impacts of decisions and actions taken now.

Potential problem and opportunity analysis consists of the following activities:

- Define the action(s) and the outcome(s) of the action(s) to be taken.

- List the associated potential issues (undesirable effects) and opportunities (desirable effects).

- Consider the causes of the potential issues and opportunities.

- Take actions to address, prevent or reduce the likely causes of potential problems and encourage the causes of opportunities.

- Prepare actions to minimise the impact of problems and maximise the impact of opportunities.

- Set triggers for contingency actions when problems or opportunities occur.

Brainstorming techniques

Brainstorming is a widely used collaborative technique that brings together a number of specialists from different areas to share ideas and discuss potential causes and alternative resolutions of a problem or set of incidents. Brainstorming can be a very productive technique enabling a problem manager to gain an insight on a problem from many different perspectives. It can be used to:

- accurately define and scope the problem;

- generate ideas;

- identify possible solutions;

- identify potential risks and issues;

- identify and agree an approach and course of action;

- define and quantify the adverse impact of any undesirable side effects;

- examine and 'walk through' alternative approaches and solutions;

- adopt a positive approach to the problem – what do we want to achieve?

- adopt a negative approach to the problem – what do we want to avoid?

A brainstorming meeting should be facilitated by the problem manager. There should be clear guidelines on what is expected from each of the participants, and it is important that:

- the right team of specialists attend the meeting;
- everyone is involved and contributes to the meeting;
- no one person dominates the meeting;
- there is no blame attributed or criticism of people or suggestions within the meeting.

During the meeting an approach to the problem and a set of actions should be agreed and documented by the problem manager and circulated to participants. The problem manager is also responsible for subsequently monitoring the progress of the agreed approach and actions. This will ensure that all actions are completed successfully in a timely fashion. If they are not, then remedial action can be taken to ensure that they are.

There are many different types of brainstorming techniques that can be used:

- **Team collaboration** – The widely used brainstorming technique described above.

- **Electronic brainstorming** – This technique uses real-time electronic meeting systems or email or shared storage systems. The advantages of this technique are that questions and suggestions can be anonymous, therefore people might be prepared to make more suggestions than they would in a face-to-face situation.

- **Directed brainstorming** – This form of brainstorming involves the use of a set of preconditions or criteria that are used to direct the brainstorming session.

- **Guided brainstorming** – This consists of a guided session around a particular topic or area within a set of constraints on time and viewpoint.

- **Individual brainstorming** – This form of brainstorming is in isolation and involves using techniques such as mind-mapping, free writing and creative thinking. All suggestions can be collected, collated and analysed. In some cases, this technique can also be more productive than traditional brainstorming techniques.

- **Question brainstorming** – This technique brainstorms a set of questions, rather than attempting to produce immediate answers and solutions.

All of these brainstorming techniques can be used to develop a set of ideas and approaches to adopt in the analysis, management and resolution of a set of incidents or a problem.

EXAMPLE – BRAINSTORMING

A service provider organisation is receiving a lot of criticism and complaints from their users and customers concerning the poor quality of service they deliver. A brainstorming meeting with representatives from many areas is called to gather all of the possible contributory causes of poor service. The following list of possible causes is obtained:

- Conflict with projects for resources
- No agreed definition of service quality
- Bureaucratic processes
- Wrong KPIs
- Confused objectives
- Poor leadership
- Lack of measurement tools
- Lack of focus on quality management
- Unreliable poor quality data
- Weak, inaccessible strategy
- Lack of integration
- Conflicting information
- Process silos
- Poor overall management tools

- Accuracy of metrics
- Inconsistent results
- Low priority for resources
- Poor resource scheduling
- Lack of service focus

These areas then become the subject of an affinity mapping exercise (see page 109) and are subsequently mapped onto an Ishikawa diagram (see page 112).

The 'five whys?' technique

The 'five whys?' is a technique that involves starting with the end result and then trying to determine the cause by asking the question 'why?' five times. It is a simple and effective method for analysing a problem and determining its root cause, and can be used in conjunction with a number of other techniques, such as brainstorming or cause-and-effect diagrams.

It can be especially useful for analysing, comparing and investigating more than one possible cause of a problem, because it allows investigation of the reasons why each cause could be responsible for the problem. It can then be used to eliminate unlikely causes and identify the most probable root cause of the scenario and its most likely resolution.

EXAMPLE – THE 'FIVE WHYS?'

Note that each of the subsequent 'Why?' questions are based on the answer to the previous 'Why?' question.

Table 4.3 Example of the 'five whys?' technique

Question	Answer
1. Why did the robot stop?	The circuit overloaded, causing a fuse to below.
2. Why is the circuit overloaded?	There was insufficient lubrication on the bearings, so they locked up.
3. Why was there insufficient lubrication on the bearings?	The oil pump on the robot is not circulating sufficient oil.
4. Why is the pump not circulating sufficient oil?	The pump intake is clogged with metal shavings.
5. Why is the intake clogged with metal shavings?	Because there is no filter on the pump.
6. Why was there no filter on the pump?	Poor design and testing process for the pump.

Note that each of the subsequent 'Why?' questions are based on the answer to the previous 'Why?' question.

The example illustrates that sometimes more than five 'why?' questions are required. It is also worth noting that the real root cause of many problems often points to a failed or missing process, therefore it might be worth changing the question from 'why?' to 'why did the process fail?' Care should be taken to focus on process failures rather than blaming people – generally it is not people who fail, but processes.

There are three key elements to the effective use of the 'five whys?' technique:

- An accurate and comprehensive definition of the problem.
- Complete honesty in answering the questions.
- Determination to get to the root cause of the problem.

The best way of using the 'five whys?' technique is to use the team approach with representatives from different areas within the organisation, and the following steps:

1. Select a team, call a meeting and agree the problem definition.
2. Ask the first question 'Why?' Record the four or five most appropriate answers.
3. For each of the answers from step 2 ask four more questions 'Why?' for each one and record each of the responses. The root cause will be obtained when a question 'Why?' has no appropriate or suitable answer. This might take more than the typical five questions and answers.
4. From the answers recorded at the lowest level (the last 'why?' question), discuss the most plausible, root causes of the problem, within the group.
5. Validate the analysis and logic of the original team with a second group.
6. After confirming the likely root cause of the problem, develop courses of action for the resolution of the problem, including the use of workarounds to reduce business disruption.
7. Select and implement the most appropriate resolutions of the root cause of the problem.

Although some people consider this a powerful tool, it has also been criticised by others as being too basic and simplistic. Reasons for this criticism include:

- ˙A tendency to stop at symptoms rather than following through to root causes.

- A tendency to stop at one root cause, whereas there could be multiple potential root causes.

- A lack of support or involvement of individuals within the team.

- An inability to identify and ask the right 'why?' questions.

- Not having the right representatives involved within the team.

However, by involving the relevant people in the right way, and validating the results obtained, it is a simple technique to use, which can produce valuable results.

A3 problem solving

The A3 technique, developed originally by Toyota, came from the principle that every issue facing Toyota could be recorded on a sheet of A3 paper. It is based around the 'Shewhart cycle' of Plan-Do-Check-Act (P-D-C-A) popularised by Demming. It can be used to develop more effective execution, planning and decision making in all areas.

There are many variants of this problem-solving report. Generally they are based upon using either six or seven stages:

- **Stage 1 Background** – In the first stage of the process, the background of the problem is described, including why it is being addressed, the business context and the business problem being analysed. It should also include the importance of the problem, the justification for its selection and an associated brief business case.

- **Stage 2 Current conditions** – This stage summarises the 'where are we now?' question. A clear and concise problem statement should be developed describing the extent and impact of the problem. This could be developed using techniques such as pain value analysis or chronological analysis.

- **Stage 3 Goal** – This stage defines the business outcome(s) required. This should be defined in terms of measurable objectives and targets.

- **Stage 4 Cause analysis** – In this stage an analysis of the current situation should be performed to determine the root cause. Problem analysis tools should be used to describe and determine the underlying root cause of the problem, such as Ishikawa diagrams (page 112), brainstorming (page 100), Kepner–Tregoe (page 95), the 'five whys?' (page 103), RCA (page 86) or other techniques.

- **Stage 5 Target conditions** – This stage defines the future required state, 'where do we want to be?' The alternative possible approaches to the problem should be considered and the best approach to adopt should be recommended.

- **Stage 6 Implementation plan** – This stage defines a brief implementation plan, summarising the actions to be taken, with owners and timescales for their implementation.

- **Stage 7 Follow up** – The final stage describes when and how the actions and plan will be evaluated and reviewed, what results should be checked, and what remaining issues and deviations could occur and how they will be dealt with, including any additional improvements that might subsequently be required.

This A3 technique is useful for developing:

- an agreed mutual definition and understanding of problems;

- focus on a problem with an agreed, common approach to its solution;

- a driver for team working and also driving improved cooperation and inter-working between teams;

- a basis for establishing a 'lean' approach to problem solving and process working;

- close links between problem solving and continual improvement.

However, the A3 technique, just like every other problem-solving technique, still requires the right people to be involved in the activity. It is also dependent upon all people accepting the content of the A3 report and completing their actions within the agreed timescales.

An example of an A3 problem-solving report template is contained within Appendix 1.

Fault isolation and replication

Fault isolation and replication involves trying to isolate a problem and then attempting to replicate it in a closely monitored and tightly controlled environment. This should preferably be an environment that has no impact on the operational services, the users or the business. This could be a development or test environment, where diagnostic tools could be used to monitor, trace and log the situation and provide more detailed information on the reason for the failure.

All of this information should provide an indication about the component or CI causing the failure and the particular areas within that particular component. This knowledge should then increase the chance of developing a workaround or a 'fix', for example by swapping out the failing component for an alternative or developing a 'patch'. If either of these techniques works, they can be tested and the solution can then be applied to the live environment using the change management process.

EXAMPLE – FAULT ISOLATION AND REPLICATION

The fault isolation and replication technique is particularly effective where the problem is a sporadic networking issue between network systems. The systems can be connected to the test network environment, and external probes, monitors or traces can then be switched and connected to the test network and the conversations between systems can be traced. These traces can be played back and analysed and this can often 'pinpoint' the exact point during the conversation where things start to go wrong, indicating:

- the chronological sequence of messages and events;
- the system causing the problem;
- the 'root cause' of the problem.

Once the problem has been observed and recorded it simplifies identification of the component at fault and will often lead to a temporary workaround or permanent resolution for the live environment. This workaround or resolution should first be verified in the test environment before being released to the live environment.

Affinity mapping

Affinity mapping and affinity diagrams are techniques used to organise large amounts of data into natural groupings. Affinity mapping was first used in the 1960s by the Japanese anthropologist Jiro Kawakita, and affinity diagrams are therefore also known as KJ diagrams or the KJ method.

Affinity mapping is particularly useful when used in conjunction with techniques such as brainstorming (page 100), that is when gathering lots of disorganised ideas. These can be written on or 'sticky' notes, which can then be stuck on walls and moved around to sort into groupings with similar attributes. Larger groups might then be sorted into subgroups, which can then be examined to see if any of them contain a 'root cause' that could explain the problem.

The steps within the affinity mapping technique can be summarised as follows:

1. Gather the information.
2. Record each idea/item on a card or 'sticky' note.
3. Look for ideas/items that are related or have similar attributes.
4. Sort ideas/items in to groups until all cards are grouped and each group is named.
5. Sort any large groups into subgroups.
6. Review the groupings, subgroupings and names.
7. Analyse the groupings looking for the most likely 'root cause(s)' or solution(s).
8. The affinity mapping/diagram can then be used to create a cause-and-effect diagram, such as an Ishikawa diagram.

Like brainstorming, the best results are often obtained when different views from many different teams or areas are sought, including stakeholders. The technique involves familiarity with the gathered information. This technique has the added benefit of leading to a deeper and better understanding of the problem and its potential solution.

EXAMPLE – AFFINITY MAPPING

This example is a continuation of the example used in the 'brainstorming' section (on page 100). In the affinity mapping exercise, each of the ideas put forward for the cause of poor quality service are written on 'sticky' notes. These notes are collected into groups and each group is given a name, as shown in Figure 4.9.

The grouping clearly demonstrates that the majority of the identified issues are associated with the definition and measurement of service quality. This indicates that this is the area to focus on first. Many of the other areas are dependent upon good quality measurements and information before improvements can be made in those areas. Once the measurements are defined and agreed, and senior management commitment is obtained, significant improvements can be made in the other areas.

Figure 4.9 Example of affinity mapping

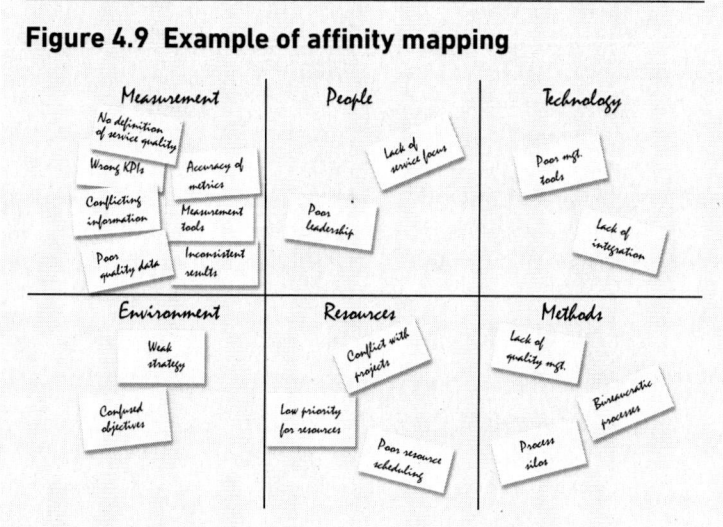

Hypothesis testing

Hypothesis testing is a technique that can be used to develop a potential statement, answer or question, which can then help to guide the direction of subsequent problem analysis and resolution. Hypotheses are early hunches, educated guesses or intuitive thoughts about the initial problem statements or questions asked about the problem, and require a clear definition of the problem to be addressed or the question to be answered. Hypotheses can often be obtained from brainstorming (see page 100) sessions.

A hypothesis needs to be a statement that can be the subject of rigorous testing. For example, if there is a problem with the speed of response from a particular server, the situation could be expressed in many ways:

- The server is overloaded.

- The network connection is too slow.

- The network connection is overloaded.

- What's wrong with the server?

The first three assertions are hypotheses that can be tested and subsequently justified or rejected. The fourth is a vague question, not a statement and cannot be tested, so it is immediately rejected.

Once a hypothesis has been formed, it is necessary to examine exactly what assertions have to be correct for the hypothesis to be correct. If any of the assertions are untrue, then the hypothesis must also be untrue or false, and can therefore be discounted.

Ishikawa diagrams

Ishikawa diagrams (sometimes called fishbone diagrams or cause-and-effect diagrams) are used to describe a useful visual technique that involves picturing the causes and effect as a 'fish skeleton'. It supports the development of a structured approach to the analysis of the probable root cause(s) of a problem and is often used in conjunction with brainstorming techniques (see page 100) to give structure to the identification and categorisation of possible causes. The method is one of the most powerful and easy to use techniques and can provide a good starting point for the use of other problem techniques. It is mainly used reactively, although again this approach can be used proactively to reduce the frequency and impact of failures and events. It can also be used to analyse processes, activities and situations and to proactively improve them.

It can help to find the resolution to a problem, to prevent it happening again or to find out:

- the cause of a desirable effect, so that it can be replicated;

- the cause of an undesirable effect, so that it can be avoided.

When something desirable happens, it is important to understand why it happened/what caused it, so that it can be made to happen again. Similarly it can be used to understand and avoid undesirable effects and their impact. If used to identify the causes of an effect it might be known as a cause-and-effect diagram. An illustration of this use is contained in the following example.

EXAMPLE – ISHIKAWA DIAGRAMS

This example is a continuation of the example used previously in the brainstorming section (on page 100) and the affinity mapping section (on page 109). The service provider organisation was receiving a lot of criticism and complaints from their users and customers, concerning the poor quality of service they were delivering. This diagram captures and records the results of the affinity mapping exercise and links the potential causes to the resulting effect.

Figure 4.10 An example of an Ishikawa diagram

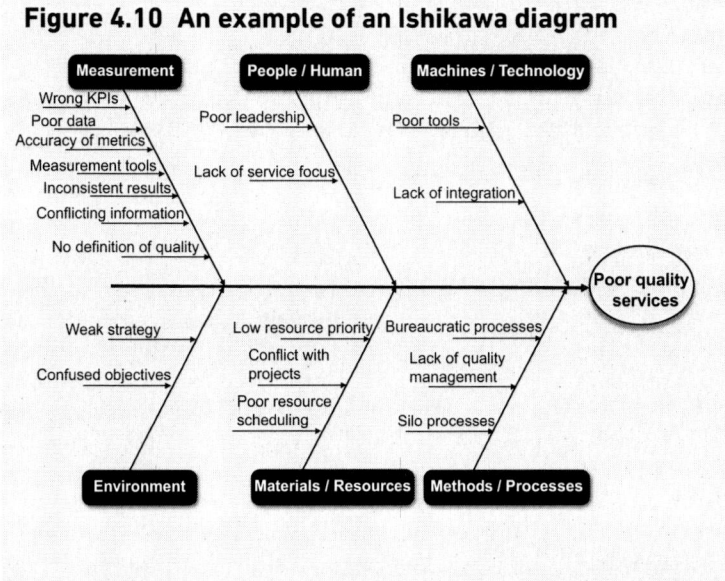

The typical categories used are:

- **Measurement** – Data and information obtained from the process that are used to govern the process and evaluate its quality and performance.
- **People/Human** – Anyone involved in the process or its management.
- **Machine/Technology** – Any equipment, technology, tools etc. that are used within the process or to manage the process.
- **Environment** – The conditions, location, office, organisation and culture in which the process operates.
- **Materials/Resources** – Finances, resources and materials required by the process.
- **Methods/Processes** – How the process is performed and governed, as well as the policies, procedures, regulations, interfaces, inputs and outputs.

There are other categories that are used in other industries such as:

- **The six Ms** – Machine, Method, Material, Manpower, Measurement and Mother nature (environment).
- **The eight Ms** – Machine, Method, Material, Manpower, Measurement, Mother nature (environment), Management/Money power and Maintenance.
- **The seven Ps** – Product (service), Price, Place, Promotion, People (personnel), Process and Physical evidence.
- **The five Ws** – Where? What? When? Who? and Why? (see page 103).

Technical observation post

The technical observation post (TOP) technique involves bringing together a group of technical specialists from the various support areas to address a particular problem or a problem area. Often this group might be called together at short notice to examine a particular problem that is occurring in real time. It is therefore better if the members of the group have been agreed beforehand.

This technique is particularly useful in three specific situations:

- When there is a critical incident or problem situation that needs to be resolved quickly in real time.

- When there is a major situation that intermittently occurs and there is no progress with resolution of the incidents or the underlying problem.

- When a major problem or set of problems is occurring and is affecting all areas of the business, but no progress is being made with its resolution.

In the first situation it is essential to bring together the appropriate group of technical specialists with the right access to the relevant services and systems. They can then monitor the sequences of events as they occur and understand and identify the underlying cause of the situation. Often by doing this and correlating the events from different systems in real time leads to a better insight into of the root cause(s) of the problem.

In the second and third situations, using a technical observation post can speed up the identification of the root cause(s) of the situation, especially where the group involves representatives from the customers, the users and also third-party partners and suppliers. Often this will provide a greater breadth of information and remove conflict and confusion. While it should be used carefully, because it can prove to be a costly exercise, it can add the following value:

- Greater profile and focus on the need and value for consistent problem management approaches.

- Improved interworking between support teams.

- Re-enforcement of the importance of knowledge and information sharing.

- Improved working relationships between the service providers and their customers, users and suppliers.

EXAMPLE – TECHNICAL OBSERVATION POST

A major financial service company has a large customer services call centre. The call centre provides a variety of services to external customers, including enquiries, support and product sales. This service is provided and supported by their internal IT organisation, as well as by two external suppliers. It is a highly complex service using computer telephony integration and bespoke in-house server and workstation software and applications. The call centre uses both in-bound and out-bound call and queue handling.

The service starts to experience issues with some of the workstations running slowly and sometimes not working altogether. Calls are made to the IT service desk, but invariably the resolution of each incident is to reboot the workstation. The call centre staff rapidly get fed up with this and just reboot their workstations when things get bad. Also service desk staff stop logging all call centre workstation incidents. A problem record is raised, but as there are only a few recurring calls and incidents, it is given a fairly low priority.

After a period of time the volume of calls handled by the call centre increases, the service deteriorates further and starts to impact not just the call centre staff, but also the service provided to the external customers. The call centre manager escalates the call to their business manager and the business manager then complains to the CIO. Problem management is asked to explain the situation.

A problem manager examines what has happened. Not only is the problem still low priority, but no one has assumed responsibility for it. The problem manager calls a TOP meeting, with representatives from all resolver groups, including representatives from the two external suppliers.

A problem description and definition is produced and agreed and potential causes of the problem are gathered. An affinity mapping exercise is completed, resulting in a cause-and-effect diagram. It is rapidly agreed that the most likely root cause of the problem is the workstation area, even though the workstation support team disagree.

Outside specialist resources get contracted in to work with the workstation support and development teams. The problem manager calls another TOP meeting with representatives from just the workstation areas and the specialist outside resource, and the process is repeated.

Actions, timescales and owners are agreed and a review meeting with the representatives from the workstation areas is arranged for early the following day. At this review meeting it is agreed that the most likely root cause is errors in the configuration of the workstation. These errors are probably causing contention between some of the workstation software. It is strongly recommended that a new workstation configuration should be built and tested. This is completed within the day and it is agreed with the call centre manager that a number of workstations will be updated to the new configuration and tested in the call centre, with on-site support from the workstation team. The most frequently failing workstations are chosen for the update. This is completed the following day and no problems are experienced with the new workstations.

All of the workstations are updated within the call centre over the following two days. The situation is reviewed daily with the call centre manager, and after a week the problem record is resolved, closed and a major problem review completed.[11]

---

[11] This review is contained in the example on page 147.

Pareto analysis

The Pareto principle (also known as the 80/20 rule, or the 'vital few' and the 'useful many') states that for many events or failures, approximately 80 per cent of the effects come from 20 per cent of the causes, as shown in Figure 4.11.

Figure 4.11 Pareto analysis

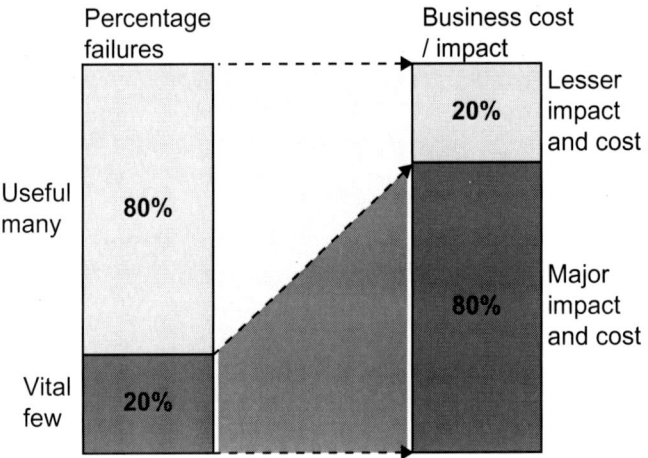

Performing a Pareto analysis supports the tackling of problems in the order of greatest benefit. Using it in conjunction with brainstorming (page 100) or the Ishikawa diagram technique (page 112) can be a very powerful tool.

A Pareto graph is a special form of vertical bar chart or column chart that allows the information to be visually displayed, as shown in Figure 4.12.

This Pareto graph plots the number of incidents for each service provided. It clearly shows that 80 per cent of incidents are attributable to just two services (the BI and Messaging services) of the ten services contained in the chart. In many

Figure 4.12 Pareto example graph

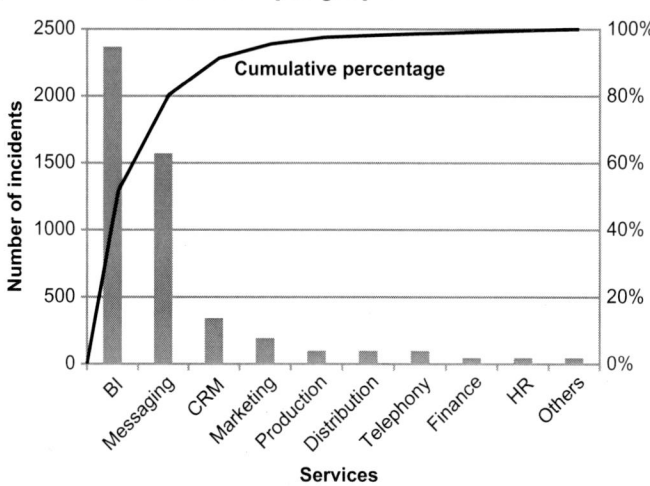

cases the identification of the 'vital few' does not come as a complete surprise, but the main benefit of using Pareto is that some major issues can be quickly demonstrated and confirmed to all concerned. Candidates for priority action, the 'vital few', appear on the left of the Pareto graph where the slope of the cumulative curve is at its steepest.

This type of analysis should really be performed on business impact or cost rather than just on plain volume. Although, if in the above example BI and Messaging are the two most business-critical services, then the real extent of the issue is revealed. The extent of the 'useful many' can sometimes be surprising too. Do not ignore the 'useful many' because items that appear trivial today might become tomorrow's big issues.

Pareto graphs can also be used to illustrate progress. Comparing Pareto graphs at key milestone points can help to evaluate the effectiveness of resolution and improvement actions. This is particularly true when it is difficult to collect specific numeric information such as issues concerning morale or customer perceptions, and subjective assessments about the 'vital few' are required.

Service failure analysis

Service failure analysis (SFA) is a technique that provides a structured approach to identifying the underlying cause of service failure events. It is based on analysing and understanding events causing the unavailability of a service or services. It might also involve the use of general management techniques, such as risk assessment, and other availability management techniques, such as component failure impact analysis (CFIA). It can be used proactively to analyse and possibly prevent future potential service failures as well as reactively to prevent failures from recurring.

SFA is based on using data from many different sources, analysing it and taking an end-to-end view of service. The key types of information for this analysis should come from:

- information from management tools on component and service failures and unavailability;
- incident management systems on incidents causing service or component unavailability;
- user and customer feedback on service issues, including complaints.

This means that it is not just technology and application issues that are considered, but also the wider management, process and support issues. Any recommendation from this analysis should be fed into the continual service improvement (CSI) process using the CSI register. Suggestions can then be assessed and prioritised with other improvement proposals, and those delivering the greatest business benefit can be selected for implementation.

SFA can be run by a problem manager as a set of activities focused on improving service availability from the business and user perspective. It can also be run as a managed programme of activity sponsored by the business, focusing on specific agreed services.

From the provider perspective the benefits of SFA are that it can be used to:

- improve the quality and value of service delivery;
- focus on key areas of business disruption and user dissatisfaction;
- change the culture of the provider organisation from a technology to a service focus;
- improve the competence, capability and knowledge of the people and the provider organisation;
- break down barriers between teams and encourage interworking.

The SFA structured approach (see Figure 4.13) can be described briefly as:

- **Identify and prioritise opportunities** – The key services to be analysed should be agreed and prioritised, based on the current level of business impact and disruption. IT and business sponsors should be agreed for each service selected within the SFA assignment. Techniques such as pain value analysis or Pareto analysis can be used to determine the appropriate priorities.

- **Plan and scope the SFA assignment** – A plan for the SFA assignment should be agreed with the sponsors before commencing with the assignment. The plan should include details of what is in and what is out of scope of the exercise. A project leader should be appointed and a project team selected from all relevant areas to ensure that all views and issues are considered.

- **Baseline the current situation** – A baseline set of measurements of the current level of 'end-to-end' service should be taken for each of the services contained within the scope of the assignment. These measurements should be taken from the business and user perspective.

- **Build hypotheses** – Probable scenarios and situations should be built and discussed with representatives from the business, representatives from the service provider management team and project team members. This can be achieved using either individual or group discussions or brainstorming techniques. The hypotheses should then be documented and agreed and input to the analysis step. Each scenario should contain a list of anticipated benefits and the associated costs.

- **Analyse data** – Once the hypotheses have been agreed, then the data to be collected can be defined and the responsibilities, methods of collection and analysis agreed. The findings of the analysis should be compared against the previously taken baseline and the hypotheses. Some potential early conclusions should be made.

- **Interview key personnel** – In parallel with the analysis, business and user representatives should be engaged and involved on a regular basis to ensure that the analysis and conclusions focus on the business and user perspective.

- **Document findings and recommendations** – Once the analysis and interviews are completed the members of the project team should meet to review and document the findings. It is important that facts and figures are gathered to evidence, justify and support each of the findings. Additional measurement and analysis might be required to achieve this and validate the findings. A set of recommended actions based on the evidence, analysis and findings of the assignment should be documented, reviewed and approved with the sponsors.

- **Implement the agreed recommendations** – A schedule of implementation for the approved recommendations should be agreed and implemented.

- **Report outcomes** – The analysis, findings and outcomes should be documented within a report, which is provided to the sponsors. This report should include a comparison of the 'before' and 'after' baselines of measurements, which will hopefully demonstrate the improvements made. An executive level summary report should also be produced for senior managers and stakeholders.

- **Benefits realisation** – The final step is to compare the actual realised benefits with the predicted benefits. Any variations between the two should be investigated and any remedial actions taken. A review of the overall assignment should also be performed to ensure that any lessons learnt are captured and stored, preferably within a service knowledge management system (SKMS) for reference by future SFA assignments. Any lessons learnt should then be reviewed and, where appropriate, suggestions fed back to other processes to ensure that systems are designed, built and tested better in the future, rather than just rectifying the situation within the operational environment.

Figure 4.13 SFA – The structured approach

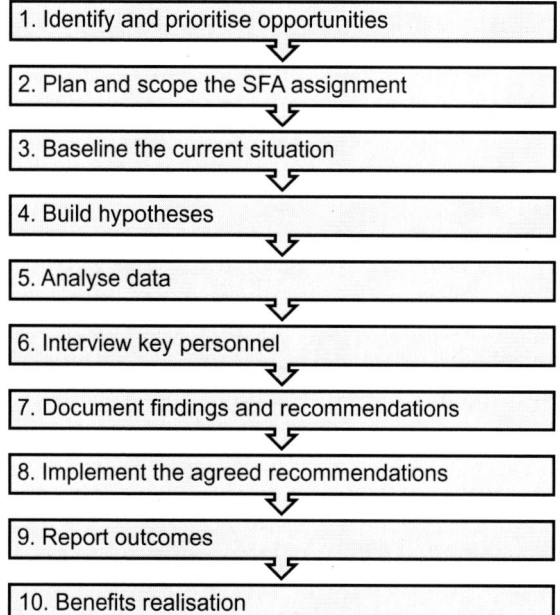

1. Identify and prioritise opportunities
2. Plan and scope the SFA assignment
3. Baseline the current situation
4. Build hypotheses
5. Analyse data
6. Interview key personnel
7. Document findings and recommendations
8. Implement the agreed recommendations
9. Report outcomes
10. Benefits realisation

EXAMPLE – SERVICE FAILURE ANALYSIS

An internal IT service provider of a retail organisation is receiving complaints from business users and customers about the availability of its services. It has three tiers of services, (tier 1 being the most important), and the current levels of service availability achieved are shown in Table 4.4.

Table 4.4 SFA example – pre-analysis

Service category	Number of services	Current availability	Current unavail- ability (monthly)	Current number of breaks per service
Tier 1	8	99.84%	7.8 hours	3.1
Tier 2	17	99.88%	9.6 hours	2.4
Tier 3	35	99.89%	18.6 hours	2.6
Total	**60**		**36.0 hours**	

Tier 1 services are failing to meet their agreed SLA availability target of 99.95 per cent. A problem manager is allocated to conduct an SFA of the tier 1 services to see if the level of availability delivered could be improved.

The following plan is agreed:

1. Recategorise incidents such that a major incident can only be raised for incidents logged that affect the availability of tier 1 services.

2. Conduct reviews and root cause analysis of all incidents affecting tier 1 service availability in the last 12 months.
3. Review recommendations from the first·two activities.
4. Prioritise the recommendations.
5. Arrange interviews and workshops with key personnel.
6. Document and agree a set of improvements.
7. Implement the improvements.
8. Measure the results.

The figures from the next 12 months are shown in Table 4.5.

Table 4.5 SFA example – post-analysis

Service category	Number of services	Current availability	Current unavail- ability (monthly)	Current number of breaks per service
Tier 1	8	99.94%	2.1 hours	1.9
Tier 2	17	99.91%	7.2 hours	2.2
Tier 3	36	99.89%	19.2 hours	2.5
Total	**61**		**28.5 hours**	

This represents a significant improvement in the availability of tier 1 services and results in a significant improvement in the level of customer satisfaction.

Component failure impact analysis

Component failure impact analysis (CFIA) is a technique used to assess and predict the impact of component failures on IT services. It is a relatively simple technique and can be used both reactively and proactively to identify single points of failure (SPoFs) and areas of weakness within the infrastructure. The technique is often performed jointly by problem managers, availability managers and continuity managers.

CFIA can be used to identify, reduce or remove:

- the dependency of services on SPoFs, including components and people;
- areas of service weakness;
- areas of high risk to service failures;
- areas of poor documentation;
- areas in need of better recovery procedures.

This information should be contained within the configuration management systems (CMS), including details of the components used and the relationships and dependencies between them.

CFIA can also provide vital feedback to the design of services from knowledge of the operational topology. The use and demand for services changes over time and components and services will often become more or less critical to the business and users they support, so the starting point for any CFIA assessment is to determine the infrastructure used to provide the service and the interdependencies between the components.

EXAMPLE – COMPONENT FAILURE IMPACT ANALYSIS

Most CMSs can produce a topological diagram of the infrastructure as illustrated in Figure 4.14.

Figure 4.14 CFIA example service topology diagram

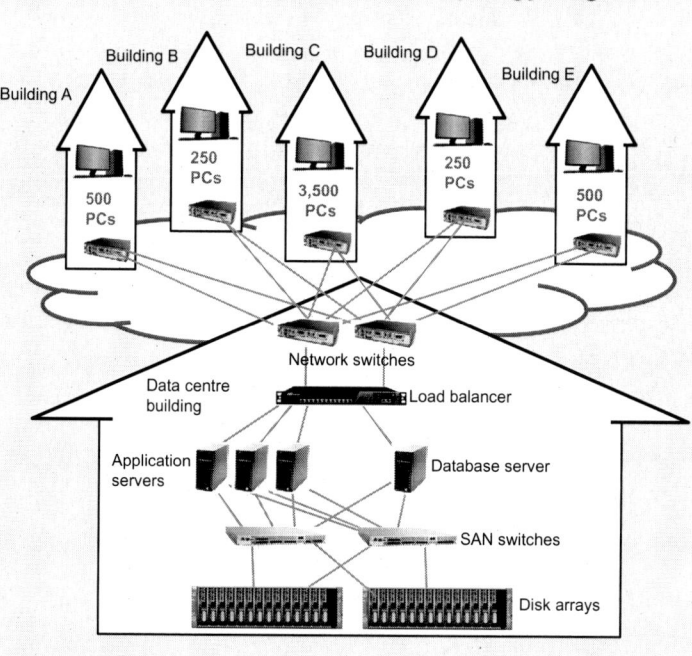

The SPoFs within the system can now be easily identified and their impact on the service can be assessed. For example, the SPoFs within the above service are:

- building A and its switch;
- building B and its switch;
- building C and its switch;
- building D and its switch;
- building E and its switch;
- the load balancer;
- the database server.

This is illustrated by the Xs in Table 4.6 for 'service A'. An 'auto' entry within the table indicates that there is an alternative component that will automatically continue to provide service if the component fails. A 'manual' entry can be used to indicate that there is an alternative component, but manual intervention is required before service can be restored. The 'weighting' column has also been included to indicate the percentage impact of the failure. In this instance it has been assumed that all PC users of the system are of equal importance.

Table 4.6 CFIA example assessment

Components	Weighting service A	Service A impact	Weighting Service B	Service B impact
Building A	10	X		
Building B	5	X		
Building C	70	X		
Building D	10	X		
Building E	5	X		
Network switch 1		Auto		
Network switch 2		Auto		
Load balancer	100	X		
Application server 1		Auto		
Application server 2		Auto		
Application server 3		Auto		

(Continued)

Table 4.6 (Continued)

Components	Weighting service A	Service A impact	Weighting Service B	Service B impact
Database server	100	X		
SAN switch 1		Auto		
SAN switch 2		Auto		
Disk arrays 1		Auto		
Disk arrays 2		Auto		

Based on this CFIA assessment we could recommend that additional resilience/recovery is considered for the following areas:

- **Priority 1** – The load balancer and the database server.
- **Priority 2** – Building C and its switch.
- **Priority 3** – Building A, B, D and E and their switches.

The priority is based on their potential impact on service availability. Failure of the load balancer or the database server will result in total service unavailability. Failure of Building C or its switch will result in 70 per cent service unavailability, whereas failure of any of the other components will result in 10 per cent or less service unavailability.

When making recommendations based on CFIA analysis, it is also worth considering the procedures for recovering a component and the time it takes for that recovery. If the recovery is simple and very quick, then this would reduce the cost-effectiveness of implementing a costly improvement.

Risk assessment and management

Even though problem managers might not be required to conduct risk assessment or management assignments, it is essential that they understand the concepts of risk and its management.

ITIL DEFINITION

Risk: A possible event that could cause harm or loss, or affect the ability to achieve objectives.

ISO/IEC 20000 DEFINITION

Risk: The effect of uncertainty on objectives.

A risk is generally measured by:

- the probability of a threat;
- the vulnerability of the asset being threatened (if applicable);
- the resulting impact if the threat occurs.

There are many types of risk assessment that can be conducted. These include the assessment of:

- **operational risk** – the assessment of the risk of failure in operational systems and services meeting their operational goals and objectives;

- **project risk** – the assessment of the risk of failure of a project or programme meeting its project goals and objectives;

- **governance risk** – the assessment of the risk of failure of governance processes meeting their goals and objectives;

- **transitional risk** – the assessment of the risk of failure of a service transition meeting its transition goals and objectives (often, closely associated with project risk).

An example of a risk assessment and management spreadsheet for the example service topology diagram in Figure 4.14 is contained in Appendix 2. This spreadsheet uses an assessment of risk based on the following formula:

Risk rating = probability × impact

where both the probability of the risk and the impact of the risk could be assessed as shown in Table 4.7.

Table 4.7 Example of the probability and impact of risk

Probability	Value	Impact	Value
Zero	0	No impact	0
Very unlikely	1	Very minor	1
Unlikely	2	Minor	2
Possible	3	Medium	3
Likely	4	Major	4
Very likely	5	Critical	5

This type of spreadsheet can be used to record the original level of risk (original risk rating) and the changed level of risk rating (current risk rating). These changes can be plotted over a period of time to reflect the improvements made in reducing risk exposure, as shown in Figure 4.15.

Figure 4.15 Example of managing risk levels

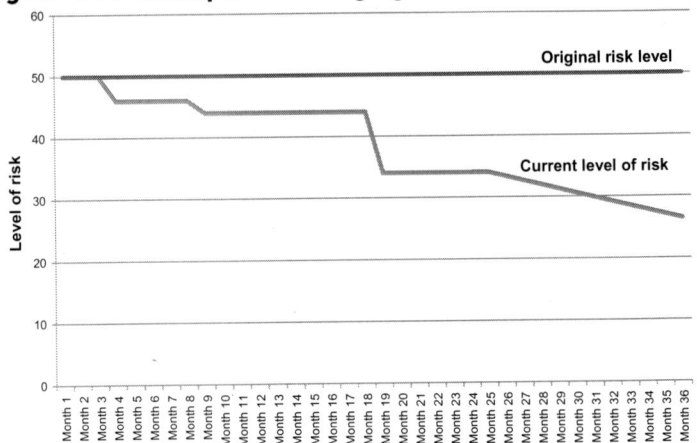

Introducing risk assessment and management practices can bring a proactive capability and focus to problem management activities. Regular use of these techniques can change the whole culture of problem management and encourage proactive thinking and action linked to continual improvement and continual learning. This then becomes the 'way of life' for problem managers.

PROBLEM CONTROL, MEASUREMENT AND REPORTING METHODS

Problem control is all about ensuring that the relevant issues are logged as problem records and that problem records are managed appropriately through a defined lifecycle to timely reduction and/or resolution. It is also about defining measurements and metrics and producing reports to demonstrate the business value of problem management activities.

Each organisation needs a clear definition of the circumstances under which a problem can be raised. Criteria need to be defined so that there is reasonable consistency in the creation and management of problem records. It might be something relatively simple, such as problem records are created for issues classified as major incidents, or when a major deviation or potential deviation from expectation is detected or anticipated. They can also be created for something more complex, such as:

- any incident with a major business impact;
- any incident affecting more than 100 users;
- any issue with more than ten related incidents.

The problem lifecycle

The lifecycle defines the set of 'status values' a problem record can have. ITIL and ISO/IEC 20000 both imply similar lifecycles for a problem record (Table 4.8).

Table 4.8 Problem lifecycles

ITIL problem lifecycle	ISO/IEC 20000 problem lifecycle
Detected	Identification
Logged	Recording
Categorised	Allocation of priority
Investigated	Classification
Diagnosed	Updating (investigation and diagnosis)
Resolved	Escalation (where appropriate)
Closed	Resolution
	Closure

However, it is also possible to operate an effective problem management process with just two status values:

- open;
- closed.

The problem manager(s) within an organisation should decide and define the most appropriate problem lifecycle that suits the requirements of the organisation. Sufficient status values should be included to enable effective management and control of problem records through the lifecycle.

Problem categorisation

One of the key areas for maintaining control of problems is the categorisation of incidents and problems. To facilitate appropriate analysis, control, management and reporting of incidents and problems, it is important that there is consistency between the categories used for the recording of incidents and those used for recording problems. In some incident and problem records a number of category fields are included:

- The type of problem, for example major or normal.
- The opening category for the incident or problem.
- The closing category for the incident or problem.

The analysis and comparison of the opening and closing categories of both incidents and problems can provide valuable management information on the effectiveness of the initial assessment of incidents and problems.

Contents of a problem record

A problem record will record the relevant information relating to a problem as it moves through the stages of its lifecycle. The typical fields contained within a problem record are:

- Unique problem number – a unique reference number.
- Problem initiator – the creator of the problem record.

- Date created – the date the problem record was created.
- Time created – the time the problem record was created.
- Problem description/problem statement – a description of the problem or the problem statement.
- Problem status – the current status of the problem.
- Opening category – the opening category of the problem.
- Closing category – the closing category of the problem.
- Business urgency – the urgency of the problem.
- Business impact – the impact of the problem.
- Priority – the priority of the problem.
- Problem symptom – the symptom(s) of the problem.
- Affected groups – business units or departments.
- Resolver group – the current resolver group responsible for diagnosing and resolving the problem.
- Problem 'bounce' count – the number of times the problem record has been bounced between different revolver groups – there should be a threshold on this count so that a problem manager is alerted when this count exceeds the accepted level.
- Problem log/history – details of all actions planned and taken to resolve the cause of the problem and the outcomes of those actions.
- Problem resolution – summary details of how the problem was resolved.
- Root cause – the root cause of the problem.

Not all of these fields are necessarily relevant to all organisations.

During its lifecycle a problem record will also have a number of relationships to other entities (Figure 4.16). The typical sorts of relationships for a problem record are:

Figure 4.16 Problem record and its relationships

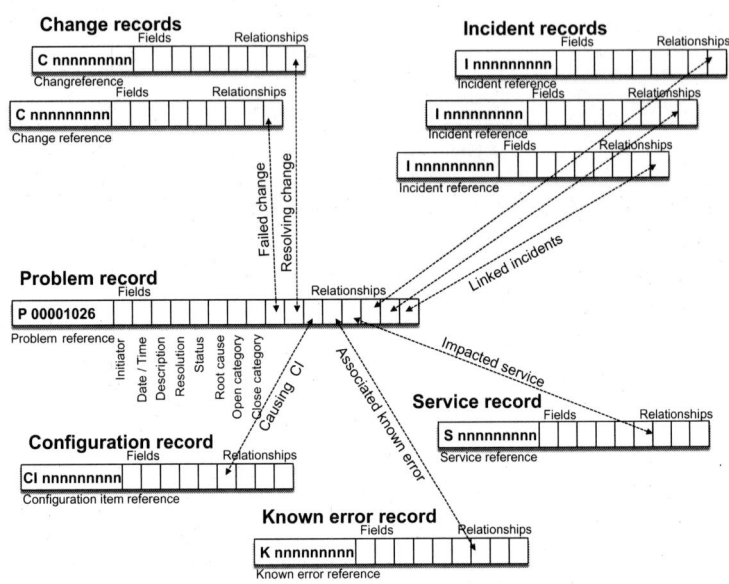

- Configuration item(s) – the main CIs causing the problem;

- Causing change – the change causing the problem, where relevant;

- Resolving change – the change(s) raised to resolve the problem;

- Service – the service(s) impacted by the problem;

- Incident – the incident(s) associated with the problem;

- Known error – the known error record(s) and workaround(s) associated with the problem.

Problem and incident escalation procedures

Problem managers should work with service desk managers and incident managers to define and maintain escalation procedures. Incident and problem escalation procedures should be agreed and consistent. Problem managers will also be involved in the actual escalation of both problems and incidents, so they need to be familiar with the content and use of escalation procedures.

There are two types of escalation procedure. These would need to be used in situations where the impact or urgency of the incident or problem had increased. The two types of escalation are:

- **Functional escalation** – If incidents or problems are threatening to breach their expected resolution targets, they will need to be escalated to the next level of technical support. This might involve escalation from second-line to third-line support or could require escalation to either a major incident or a major problem. This action might then necessitate using crisis management procedures or even invocation of continuity plans in extreme situations. If third-party suppliers are involved this could also require hierarchical escalation to senior managers.

- **Hierarchical escalation** – This involves escalating the incident or problem to the next level of management. Again this is most likely to occur if the incident or problem is taking too long to diagnose or resolve. Hierarchical escalation should then continue up the 'management chain' if the situation is not resolved.

In each of these situations the conditions for escalation to the various levels, and the paths, communication methods and contact points, need to be agreed and documented. Problem managers need to be familiar with these procedures so that they can take the appropriate action when required.

Often problem managers are involved in the management and control of major incidents and problems. Sometimes, in order to minimise the impact of a major incident or problem, it will be necessary to invoke business and/or IT recovery plans. Problem managers should therefore be familiar with business continuity management (BCM) and IT service continuity management (ITSCM) procedures and plans to ensure they understand how these activities will be instigated. Problem managers also need to ensure that incident and problem escalation procedures are consistent with BCM and ITSCM procedure and plans.

Problem and incident arbitration

Arbitration processes are needed when there is discussion or disagreement around the responsibility for the investigation, diagnosis or resolution of an incident or problem. Sometimes incident records and problem records will 'bounce' between resolver groups, which can result in delays in the response and resolution activities. Problem managers should work with incident managers and service desk managers to ensure that these situations happen rarely and that, when they do happen, they are quickly identified and rapidly resolved.

To do this, problem managers should arrange a review meeting or a 'brainstorming' session with the relevant resolver groups. During this meeting, a set of actions and timescales should be agreed with owners to ensure that the agreed user and customer targets and expectations can be met.

Measurements and metrics

There are many measurements and metrics that can be used to measure the effectiveness and efficiency of the problem management process. However, often it is much more effective to focus on one or two key metrics than to use a multitude of measurements.

Both ITIL and COBIT® propose some potential KPIs and metrics that could be used by problem management.

ITIL suggests a number of critical success factors (CSFs) and key performance indicators (KPIs) for problem management. Each CSF is listed with a number of associated KPIs. Each organisation should select a set of CSFs and KPIs that are appropriate for them. The list of suggested CSFs and KPIs is summarised in the Table 4.9.

Table 4.9 Summary of the ITIL CSFs and KPIs

CSF: Minimise business impact:

- Number of known error records raised
- Number of inaccuracies within the KEDB
- Percentage of calls resolved at the first point of contact by the service desk

CSF: Maintain IT service quality

- The number of problems raised per period
- The length of the problem backlog
- The number of recurring incidents

CSF: Maintain problem management capability and deliver service quality

- Percentage of problems wrongly assigned or categorised
- The numbers and trends in the number of problems and the problem backlog
- The average cost of a problem

COBIT® groups problem management metrics in terms of either an IT-related goal or a process-related goal. The list of metrics are summarised in Tables 4.11 (on page 176) and 4.12 (on page 178).

Too many measurements are often used, and the focus and intent of the measurements are lost. The metrics selected should always try to measure the quality of the process outcome(s) rather than the process output(s). These outcomes should be measured from the perspective of the business, customer and user. However, in the initial stages of establishing a problem management process this is difficult, if not impossible to do. The capability of a relatively immature process will not support this level of sophistication, so other metrics will need to be used. This illustrates a very important aspect of KPIs and metrics: they need to be reviewed on a regular basis to ensure that the most appropriate metrics are being used.

If the main objective of the problem management process is to minimise the business disruption caused by incidents and problems on an organisation, then the most appropriate metrics to use to monitor the effectiveness of the problem management process are:

- the total business impact/disruption caused by incidents and problems per time period (e.g. per month);
- the total number of open problems without an acceptable known error and workaround.

These two metrics give a reasonable indication of the amount of pain or disruption being experienced by the business. While these are very difficult KPIs or metrics to calculate, they represent the quality of the process outcome in relation to the main objective. However, for these metrics to work, a mature problem management process is required, as well as many other mature IT and business processes. If the appropriate levels of process maturity are not there, then an indicative KPI or metric can initially be used, such as one of the following:

- the total volumes of incidents and problems;
- the total volumes of major incidents and major problems;
- the volume and duration of major incidents and major problems;
- the volume and duration of incidents and problems causing service unavailability;
- the total cost of problem resolution;

- the volume and duration of incidents and problems causing unavailability of critical services.

The list is in increasing order of the process maturity required.

Other commonly used metrics are:

- the total outstanding backlog of problems;
- the number of problems resolved within the agreed elapsed time.

It should be recognised that the targets, KPIs and metrics that are used will actually influence the attitude and behaviour of the personnel involved in the process, for example it might drive them to focus on lesser priority problem records to meet targets or to close problem records when the root cause of the problem has not been fully resolved. Therefore, extreme care should be exercised when using and publicising the use of any targets, KPIs and metrics.

Reporting

Problem management reporting is an important activity that should be used to:

- drive the right behaviours;
- keep the focus of the process and activities on the key areas;
- intervene when things deviate from expectation;
- measure the impact of changes and improvements;
- publicise achievements and successes.

The reporting activity and reports for problem management consist of fulfilling the need:

- for measuring KPI(s) associated with achieving the main objective(s) of problem management;

- of the problem management process and activities;
- of other processes and activities.

Before problem management activities are established within an organisation the only reporting opportunities available to a problem manager are those associated with incidents and incident management. By analysing the types and volumes of incidents that occur within the organisation, problem managers can determine which areas to address first. They can then apply 'pain value' analysis or Pareto analysis techniques to analysis those areas causing the greatest business disruption (see pages 93 and 118).

Another report, as shown in Figure 4.17, shows the number of major incidents and the total number of incidents occurring over a period of time. From this graph it can be seen that the total number of incidents has not changed significantly. It remains around 4,000 per month. However, during this period the number of major incidents has increased dramatically, from just under 100 (around 2 per cent) to almost 500 per month (around 12 per cent). This could indicate a significant rise in the amount of disruption being experienced by the business, customers and users.

Figure 4.17 Incident and major incident volumes

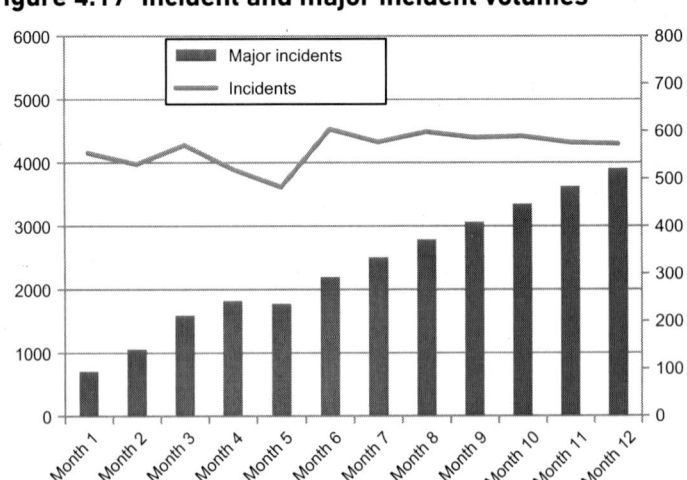

Other types of reports can be used to analyse the trends associated with incidents. The graphs in Figures 4.18 and 4.19, from two different organisations, illustrate this.

The graph in Figure 4.18 points to a potentially improving situation where the average number of closed incidents is exceeding the number of opened incidents, which means

Figure 4.18 Incident volumes and backlogs: organisation 1

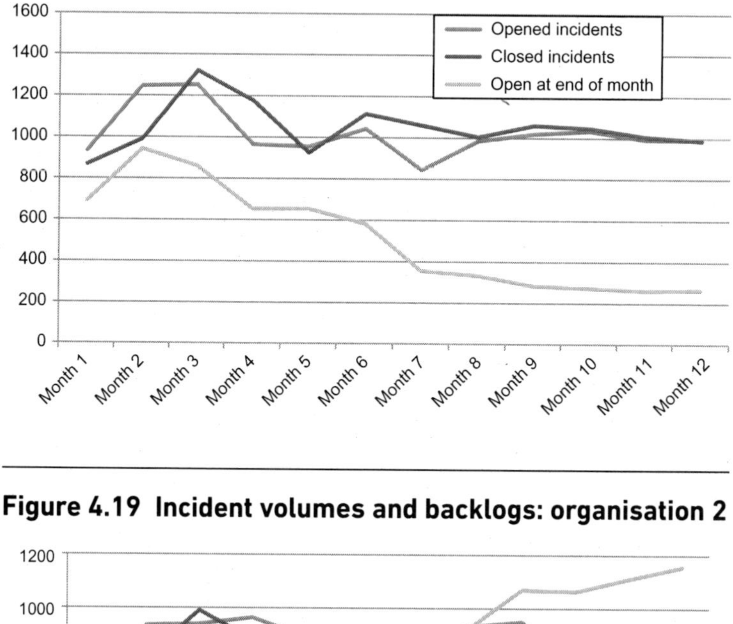

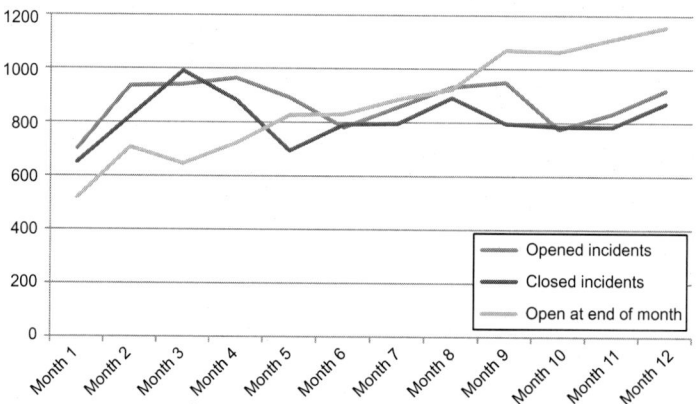

Figure 4.19 Incident volumes and backlogs: organisation 2

the backlog of incidents is decreasing. The graph in Figure 4.19 indicates a potential problem situation where things are worsening because the average number of closed incidents is less than the number of opened incidents and the backlog has doubled over a period of 12 months. If this situation is not addressed soon the number of complaints is likely to increase, if it hasn't already.

Once problem management processes are established and problem records start to be created, similar graphs can be produced for problem volumes and backlogs.

These reports and techniques are useful for trying to establish some 'quick wins' by addressing those areas of greatest pain and disruption. However, remember these are only indicators, and stakeholder and customer comment, feedback and complaints should also be acted upon.

As the problem management process matures and the capability grows, reports can be changed to give greater focus on the business and customer perspective. Some of the reports that can be produced are illustrated in Figures 4.20 and 4.21.

The graph in Figure 4.20 shows the current 'top ten' problem records. The bars in the graph show the total incident count for each problem. The line on the graph shows the number of incidents recorded for each of those problem records. These indicate that the top two problem records (PR 1736 and PR 2362) have probably had the greatest impact over the last week. This type of analysis can also be done on matching incidents to identify those sets of incidents that are having the greatest impact, but have not yet had a problem record raised.

The graph in Figure 4.21 indicates the estimated business disruption caused by incidents and problems. This type of graph is useful for driving attitude and culture within an organisation as well as ensuring that the focus of problem management activities remains on the business and customer outcomes.

Figure 4.20 The current 'top ten' problems

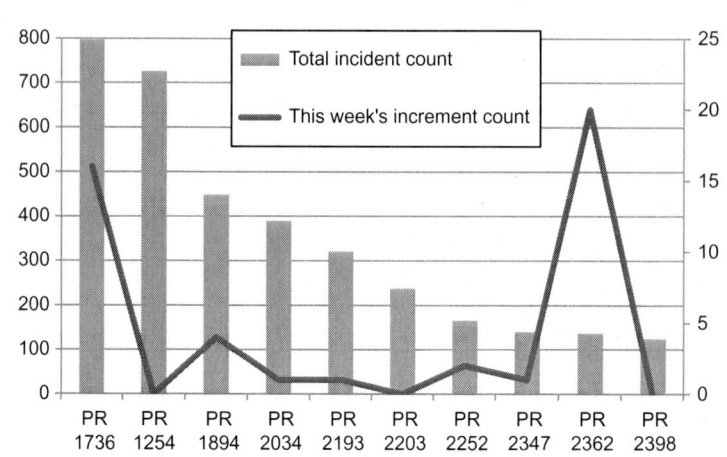

Figure 4.21 Estimated monthly business disruption from incidents and problems

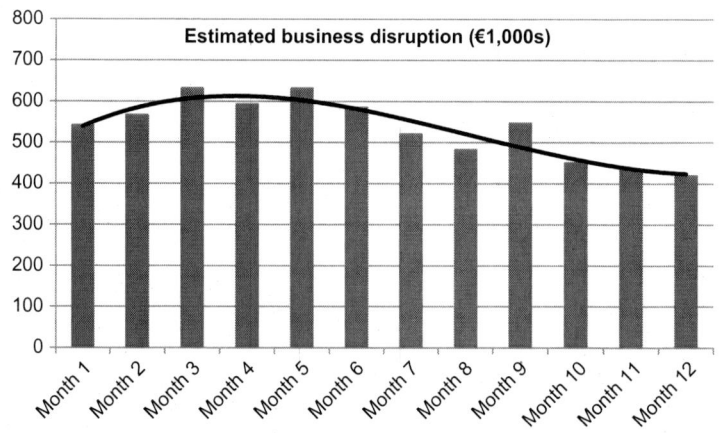

MAJOR PROBLEM REVIEWS

There are two types of major problem review (MPR) meetings:

- **Closure** – These should be conducted before the closure of any major problem record, once the problem has been satisfactorily resolved and service has been completely restored.

- **Interim** – These might be called to review progress to date on serious ongoing problems, especially those that have open incidents or open major incident records linked to them.

Often problem managers are asked to conduct post-incident reviews and post-implementation reviews (PIRs) as well as MPRs, and in some organisations these review meetings are conducted at the same time. This means the reports from all of these reviews should be similar: however, it should be remembered that the objectives of the associated activities are different:

- The objective of incident management activities is the restoration of normal service as soon as possible.
- The objective of problem management activities is the permanent resolution of the underlying root cause of the problem.
- The objective of change management activities is the implementation of successful changes.

Problem review meetings should be conducted by experienced problem managers. They need to include representatives from all of the groups involved with the problem, including any third parties. They should be well planned, well facilitated and well documented using a standard review meeting template. (An example of an MPR template is contained in Appendix 3.)

All review meetings should be documented and should record:

- a summary of the problem and the actions taken;
- why the problem occurred;
- any lessons learnt;
- any opportunities for improvement;
- any subsequent follow-up actions required;

- any necessary actions to prevent a recurrence;
- any further training or education needed;
- any additional documentation or information required.

The biggest issue to avoid when running review meetings is that of apportioning blame. It is important to focus on the positive aspects, learn from the mistakes and prevent anyone else within the organisation from repeating the experience.

Ideally, many of the 'lessons learnt' from review meetings should be recorded as knowledge articles within the service knowledge management system (SKMS). By adopting this approach, review meetings can provide a vital source of information to proactive problem management.

Closure MPRs

Once a major problem has been resolved and before the problem record is closed, a formal MPR should be completed. The review should record:

- why and how the situation occurred;
- a review of what was done and when;
- things that were done well;
- things that were done badly;
- things that could be done better next time;
- how to prevent recurrence;
- any necessary follow-up actions;
- any lessons learnt for the future.

EXAMPLE – MAJOR PROBLEM REVIEW

This example is a summary of the key areas of the review of the major problem described in the TOPs section (on page 114).

- Why and how did the situation occur?
  - The configuration of the workstation was incorrect.
  - There was a lack of engagement with the call centre manager and the call centre agents.
- What was done and when?
  - January – a new workstation build was released to the call centre.
  - February – issues with the new workstations start occurring.
  - March – components of the workstation build were updated.
  - April – a member of the workstation team attends an on-site meeting with the call centre manager.
  - May – additional components of workstation build were updated.
  - June – again a workstation team member visits the call centre manager.
  - July – the call centre manager's manager rings the CIO and escalates the problem.
- Things that were done well:
  - The resolution of the problem, once it was escalated.
- Things that were done badly:
  - The volume and trend of incidents was not recognised.
  - The problem was not recognised as serious and was not escalated soon enough.
- Things that could be done better next time:
  - Analysis of volumes and trends of incidents on a regular basis.
  - Review the progress and priority of outstanding problems on a regular basis.

- Defining better escalation processes and escalate to major problems earlier when appropriate.
- How to prevent recurrence:
  - Implement improved processes for building, testing and releasing workstation releases.
  - Implement improved incident and problem management processes.
- Necessary follow-up actions:
  - Design and implement new processes for building, testing and releasing workstation releases.
  - Design and implement new processes for incident and problem management.
- Lessons learnt for the future:
  - Ensure that frequent and regular engagement with the call centre manager and agents occurs.
  - Ensure that all calls to the call centre are logged as incidents.
  - Improve release, incident and problem management processes and procedures.
  - Improve the skills and knowledge of the workstation team and the call centre team. ·
  - Improve incident and problem management measuring, trending and reporting.

Interim MPRs

Interim MPRs might be held to investigate unresolved, unusual or high impact problems. They might be conducted on problem records that have been escalated or that have associated open incident records. In this case the problem manager conducting the interim MPR must ensure that the MPR does not impede the progress of the analysis and resolution activities for any incident or problem. Rather, the MPR should help to expedite these activities by reviewing the events, actions and progress to date; revising and amending any future actions based on the history of the problem; and producing a revised schedule of actions and owners.

Sometimes problem managers are involved in or manage major incident crisis meetings. These are often held when a major incident is causing massive disruption to an organisation. The techniques used to run the meeting are similar to those used to run PIRs and MPRs. However, the problem manager must remember in these meetings that the focus must always remain on restoration of normal service as soon as possible. All discussions and actions must be concentrated on restoring an agreed level of acceptable service to the users and customers as soon as possible.

Problem managers should work with the service desk and incident management to agree and document a crisis procedure for major incidents. This procedure should be documented and all problem managers should be familiar with its operation. It should have clearly defined links with the business and IT continuity and recovery plans and their invocation.

Crisis meetings should be held regularly during the resolution of a major incident. They should bring together representatives from the required areas of expertise to agree action plan(s), responsibilities and timescales and a schedule for future crisis meetings to review and revise the agreed action plan(s). Some organisations have a crisis meeting room allocated for such an eventuality.

PROACTIVE PROBLEM MANAGEMENT

The objective of proactive problem management is defined in ITIL as:

> ...to identify problems that might otherwise be missed. Proactive problem management analyses incident records and uses data collected by other IT service management processes to identify trends or significant problems.

This can be achieved by collating, analysing and trending data and information from other processes to prevent the occurrence of avoidable failures and incidents.

In many organisations proactive problem management doesn't happen, the reason being that problem managers and problem management resources are scarce and demands for reactive activities are always a higher priority. The only way to overcome this issue is to ring-fence some problem management resource, for instance one problem manager or 20 per cent of a problem manager's time (a day a week) to be spent dedicated to proactive problem management activity. This role could then be rotated throughout the problem management team so that all problem managers adopt a proactive approach to the way they work. If this capability can also be transferred to personnel within resolver groups and other areas, then the attitude and culture of the whole organisation starts to change.

The following are some potential proactive problem management activities:

- Using proactive monitoring to look at patterns of events to predict possible future failures, for example through warnings, tolerances and thresholds. These events can help to detect abnormal components, services, patterns or usage that are outside acceptable operating levels.

- Using 'autonomation' techniques, by learning from past experience and working with event management, using the analysis and collation of events to predict and/or prevent avoidable failures. The monitoring and the response/alerting should be automated wherever possible, with only exceptions being escalated for manual intervention.

- Using incident analysis and trending techniques, so that the root cause of the underlying problem(s) associated with frequently occurring incidents can be identified and resolved.

- Working closely with availability management and capacity management, using techniques such as SFA, CFIA or risk assessment and management to identify SPoFs, areas of poor performance, areas of weakness.

- Working closely with SACM to identify CIs within the CMS that cause failures or have high numbers of associated incident and problem records.

- Identifying and resolving incidents and problems in one area, component, system or service, and reviewing all other areas, components, systems or services to see if it is appropriate and cost-effective to apply the resolutions to those as well.

- Raising problem records, change requests or improvement suggestions wherever potential failure issues, events and situations might arise.

- Making improvements to the problem management process and techniques, and assisting with instigating improvements in other processes and techniques.

- Using information and knowledge sharing, linked with continual learning, to develop and improve capability in all areas continually.

- Ensuring that problem records are raised or improvement suggestions are recorded in the CSI register, where proactive actions are identified that could resolve a potential issue or could improve the quality of a service.

- Ensuring that 'lessons learnt' from problem activities, especially MPRs, are recorded as knowledge articles within the SKMS and are publicised to all relevant personnel.

- Ensuring that opportunities for improvement identified within MPRs are input to service reviews and the CSI register.

EXAMPLE – PROACTIVE PROBLEM MANAGEMENT

During their weekly meeting the service desk manager and the problem manager are discussing incident resolution times. Although the incident resolution report indicates that the organisation is achieving its incident resolution targets, the incident manager is concerned that a number of incidents are taking a long time to be resolved.

By going through the incident log and the comments and updates recorded for these incidents, the problem manager finds that these incidents are constantly being 'bounced' from one resolver group to another. A quick change to the incident management system is implemented to record the number of times an incident record is 'bounced' from one resolver group to another and the name of each resolver group involved. This reveals that some of the incidents are bounced between different resolver groups over 40 times before being resolved.

The incident manager and problem manager present their findings to all of the resolver groups. The incident management system is modified and a limit is imposed on a 'bounce count' for every incident. Any incident bouncing more than five times will alert the problem manager, who will review the situation with the resolver groups concerned. A resolver group owner is agreed, who is responsible for the resolution of the incident. If this needs to change it has to be justified and agreed with the problem manager before the incident can be transferred to a new owning resolver group.

These changes resulted in:

- an improved service to the business;
- a significant reduction in incident resolution times for users and customers;

- a large reduction in wasted time and resolver group resources (it took approximately 2 minutes of resolver effort at each 'bounce');
- a reduction in delays (each 'bounce' resulted in a 4-hour delay on average);
- cost savings from reduced volumes of incidents by some suppliers.

The other major benefit was that this activity significantly increased the credibility and profile of both the problem manager and the problem management process.

REVIEW AND AUDIT OF PROBLEM MANAGEMENT ACTIVITIES

The problem management process, procedures and activities should be regularly reviewed and audited. Reviews should be completed at least annually. The objective of these reviews is to ensure that processes and procedures are complied with and to identify areas of weakness or opportunities for improvement. These reviews can be completed by someone working within the problem management process, such as the problem management process owner or manager, or by external specialists.

Process audits should also be completed on a regular basis, but should be conducted by someone independent of the process, such as an internal or external auditor. The objective of these audits is to identify areas of non-compliance. Areas of non-compliance should be recorded as improvement actions for remedial action as soon as possible.

USE OF PROBLEM MANAGEMENT TECHNIQUES

Table 4.10 summarises where the main benefits will be gained from the application of the methods and techniques within the principal activities of problem management.

Table 4.10 Use of the problem management techniques

Problem definition	Problem prioritisation	Problem investigation and analysis	Identification of workarounds	Problem diagnosis	Root cause analysis	Proactive problem management
Creative problem solving	Pain value analysis	Creative problem solving	Use of known errors, workarounds and knowledge articles	Chronological analysis	Root cause analysis	Service failure analysis
Kepner–Tregoe	Pareto analysis	Chronological analysis		Brainstorming	5 Whys	Component failure impact analysis
Mind mapping	Brainstorming	5 Whys		Hypothesis testing	Hypothesis testing	Risk assessment and management
Brainstorming		Brainstorming		Kepner–Tregoe	Kepner–Tregoe	Major problem review
A3 problem solving		Hypothesis testing		Fault isolation	Brainstorming	Review and audit

(Continued)

Table 4.10 (Continued)

Problem definition	Problem prioritisation	Problem investigation and analysis	Identification of workarounds	Problem diagnosis	Root cause analysis	Proactive problem management
		Kepner–Tregoe		Affinity mapping	Fault isolation	
		Mind mapping		Ishikawa diagrams	Affinity mapping	
		A3 problem solving		Technical observation post	Ishikawa diagrams	
		Fault isolation			Technical observation post	
		Affinity mapping				
		Ishikawa diagrams				
		Technical observation post				

STANDARDS AND FRAMEWORKS

This section describes and explains the problem management material contained within the key IT service management standards and frameworks.

Standards

ISO/IEC 20000 is the international standard for service management. The standard provides details of a set of processes contained within a service management system that should be established for the effective delivery of IT services. It can also be used as a reference for review, audit and possible certification to a defined level of capability.

It is a multipart standard consisting of several documents:

- Part 1: Information technology – Service management – Part 1: Service management system requirements (ISO/IEC 20000-1:2011).

- Part 2: Information technology – Service management – Part 2: Guidance on the application of service management systems (ISO/IEC 20000-2:2012).

- Part 3: Information technology – Service management – Guidance on scope definition and applicability of ISO/IEC 20000-1 (ISO/IEC 20000-3:2012).

- Part 4: Information technology – Service management – Process reference model (ISO/IEC TR 20000-4:2010).

- Part 5: Information technology – Service management – Exemplar implementation plan for ISO/IEC 20000-1 (ISO/IEC TR 20000-5:2010).

- Part 10: Information technology – Service management – Concepts and terminology for ISO/IEC 20000-1 (ISO/IEC TR 20000-10).

The most relevant documents with respect to problem management are Parts 1 and 2. The framework of the IT service management system (IT SMS) and the processes contained within the standard are shown in Figure 4.22.

Figure 4.22 The ISO/IEC 20000 processes

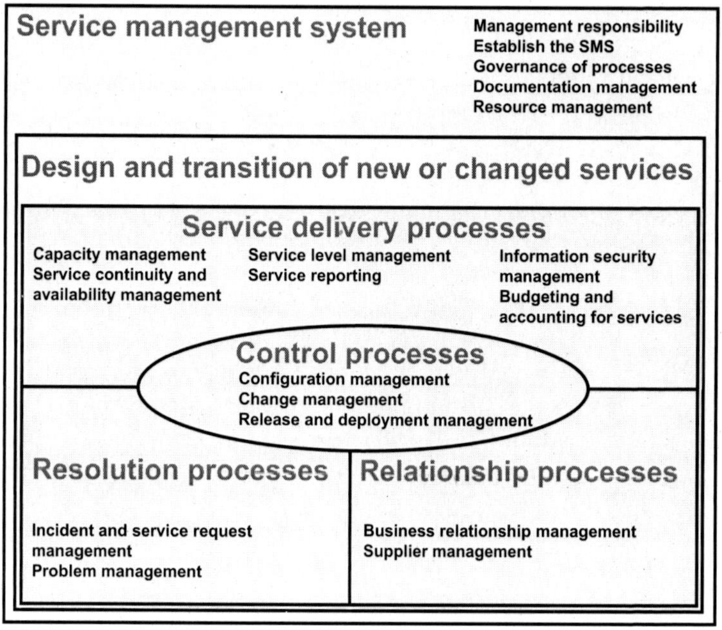

| Service management system | Management responsibility
Establish the SMS
Governance of processes
Documentation management
Resource management |

Design and transition of new or changed services

Service delivery processes

| Capacity management
Service continuity and availability management | Service level management
Service reporting | Information security management
Budgeting and accounting for services |

Control processes
Configuration management
Change management
Release and deployment management

| **Resolution processes** | **Relationship processes** |
| Incident and service request management
Problem management | Business relationship management
Supplier management |

Part 1 of the ISO/IEC 20000 standard details those areas considered essential for effective management within each of the process areas. By using this information an organisation can focus on and prioritise the key areas for implementing an effective problem management process.

Problem management is one of the two resolution processes within ISO/IEC 20000, the other being incident management. The following information is an extract from section 8, of Part 1 of the standard (the resolution processes), on the problem management process:

There shall be a documented procedure to identify problems and minimise or avoid the impact of incidents and problems. The procedure for problems shall define:

a. identification
b. recording
c. allocation of priority
d. classification
e. updating of records
f. escalation
g. resolution
h. closure.

Problems shall be managed according to the procedure.

The service provider shall analyse data and trends on incidents and problems to identify root causes and their potential preventive action.

Problems requiring changes to a CI shall be resolved by raising a request for change.

Where the root cause has been identified, but the problem has not been permanently resolved, the service provider shall identify actions to reduce or eliminate the impact of the problem on the services. Known errors shall be recorded.

The effectiveness of problem resolution shall be monitored, reviewed and reported.

Up-to-date information on known errors and problem resolutions shall be provided to the incident and service request management process.

Part 2 of the standard provides further guidance on the application of service management process. It contains the following information, under five headings, on the problem management process, within the resolution processes in section 8 of the standard.

Intent of the requirements

The problem management process identifies the unknown, underlying root causes of incidents and proposes permanent resolutions through the change management process. The problem management process also proactively prevents incidents from occurring through trend analysis and recommendations of preventative action.

Concepts

The problem management process should investigate the root causes of incidents. The problem management process should then minimise or avoid the impact of incidents and problems through proposing permanent solutions via the change management process.

The problem management process should also produce and manage the known error records including temporary fixes once the underlying root cause has been identified. The known error records can be used to ensure efficient incident resolution and organisational learning.

The problem management process should have a defined scope and should determine the problem management methods used. It can be useful to have a problem management policy that can define the criteria for both prioritisation and investigation of problems.

The primary focus of the problem management process for many organisations is based upon incidents that have already occurred. There can be tremendous benefit to the organisation in finding permanent resolutions for the highest impact and highest risk problems, which in turn can enable the services to become more reliable, cost-effective and efficient.

Once the environment has become more reliable as a result of these problem management activities, it might be possible for personnel to spend more time on proactive problem management. Proactive problem management activities should be aimed at preventing incidents from occurring in the first place. For example, identifying a potential single point of failure for a business critical service and proposing redundancy to prevent any future incident impacting the customer.

Explanation of requirements

The problem management process should include the procedures listed below.

    a.   Problem identification, including:

        1. detection of an unknown root cause of one or more incidents;

        2. the analysis of one or more incidents revealing an underlying problem;

        3. a notification from a supplier or an internal group of a problem with a component of the service.

    b.   Problem recording, to ensure that each problem is recorded. The records should include relevant details of the problem, including the date and time, and a cross-reference to the incident(s) that initiated the problem record.

    c.   Problem classification and prioritisation, which should ensure that:

        1. each problem is categorised to help determine its nature and to provide meaningful information, making use of the same classification criteria that are used in the incident and service request management process;

2. each problem is given a priority for resolution according to its urgency and the impact of related incidents;

3. time and resources for investigating the problem and identifying the best options for resolution are allocated according to the priority of the problem;

4. the resolution of the problem is allocated time and resources according to the priority of the problem and the benefit of making the change in order to fulfil service requirements.

d. Problem investigation and diagnosis, which should ensure that:

1. each problem is investigated to diagnose the root cause;

2. a method of resolution can be identified, which depends on the impact of related incident(s) and potential incidents, whether or not a temporary fix exists and the estimated cost of resolution;

3. a decision to resolve the problem depends on the impact of related incidents, whether a temporary fix exists and the cost of resolution;

4. a decision not to resolve the problem is managed according to the problem management policy;

5. the problem management process is able to support the incident and service request management process even before the known error is found, through identifying a temporary fix;

6. problem diagnosis is complete when the root cause is identified and a method of resolving the problem is identified.

e. Problem tracking should ensure that the progress of all problems is recorded:

1. to track the progress through the problem management process, including details of the person currently responsible for progressing the problem;

2. to record all resources used and actions taken.

f. Problem escalation should ensure all issues are escalated to appropriate parties including:

1. identification of related incident(s) breaching service targets;

2. cascading information to the customer so they can take appropriate actions to minimise the impact of the unresolved problem;

3. enable the service desk or level 1 support to provide regular updates to affected users or customers;

4. defining the escalation points.

g. Documenting known errors, which should ensure that:

1. when the root cause and a proposed method of resolving the problem is identified, a known error is recorded in the known error database, together with details of any temporary fix;

2. a known error record is not closed until after the permanent solution has been successfully implemented via the change management process;

3. known error records are made available to all relevant personnel and they are regularly made aware of any new or updated known error records;

4. if a known error record stays open for a defined duration of time, it is reviewed and kept up to date so that no obsolete information is held in the known error database;

5. all known errors are recorded against the current and potentially affected services and the configuration item suspected of being at fault.

h. Problem record closure, when the known error has been identified and recorded, should ensure that:

1. details of resolution have been accurately recorded;

2. the problem record has been matched to any related incidents to facilitate analysis;

3. the root cause is categorised to facilitate analysis.

i. Major problem reviews held to investigate unresolved, unusual or high impact problems, should ensure:

1. risks to the business, the customer or service provider are identified and managed;

2. there is management visibility into the reasons for unresolved problems, as well as their ongoing business impact.

j. Problem reviews should be recorded and should include appropriate recommendations for improvements to the service. They should examine:

1. opportunities to improve the problem management process;

2. opportunities to improve other processes, services or the SMS;

3. how to prevent recurrence of a particular type of problem;

4. whether training or awareness should be provided to correct or prevent incidents caused by human error;

5. whether there has been any responsibility on the part of suppliers, customers or internal groups for problems that have occurred and whether any follow-up actions are required.

k. Proactive problem management should ensure that:

1. incident and problem data, the CMDB and other relevant information sources are analysed to identify trends;

2. incident and problem data, the CMDB and other relevant information sources can be used to improve decision making and assist with pre-empting possible degradations of service;

3. the knowledge gained from a problem review is communicated to the customer to ensure that the customer is aware of the actions taken and the service improvement recommendations identified;

4. key measurements that demonstrate the business value of proactive problem management are defined;

5. potential single points of failure, emerging trends and risks to services are identified and options are proposed through the change management process.

Documents and records

The documents and records that should be produced and retained by the problem management process should include:

a. problem management procedures;

b. problem records;

c. known error records;

d. details of temporary fixes;

e. links to changes resulting in permanent fixes;

f. problem review records including minutes of problem review meetings;

g. management reports including incident and problem trend information;

h. recommendations for service improvements.

A problem management policy can be useful to facilitate and support the problem management process.

Authorities and responsibilities

In addition to the process owner, process manager and personnel performing the procedures of the process as described in [Clause 4.4.2.1], authorities and responsibilities required within the problem management process should include:

a. personnel who carry out the root cause analysis of problems, determine the resolution and/or temporary fix and create the associated known error data record;

b. suppliers, customers or internal groups involved in providing resolutions, temporary fixes, known error information, advice and reviews.

Best practice frameworks, procedures and processes

The ISO/IEC standard provides details on a set of requirements that need to be met in order for a service provider organisation to manage and deliver IT services effectively. The standard provides details of 'what' has to be put in place for effective IT service delivery. Frameworks such as ITIL and COBIT® generally provide information on 'how' this can actually be achieved. They provide information on the goals, the objectives, the processes and the metrics that need to be in place in order to meet the requirements contained within the ISO/ISO 20000 standard. These two frameworks, ITIL and COBIT®, can be used together as complementary frameworks and are explained in greater detail in the following two subsections.

ITIL

ITIL is a set of books containing guidance on service management best practice. It contains five core books, one on each stage of the service lifecycle:

- ITIL (2011) Service Strategy. ISBN: 9780113313044
- ITIL (2011) Service Design. ISBN: 9780113313051
- ITIL (2011) Service Transition. ISBN: 9780113313068
- ITIL (2011) Service Operation. ISBN: 9780113313075
- ITIL (2011) Continual Service Improvement. ISBN: 9780113313082

ITIL defines a complete lifecycle approach to service management, consisting of five lifecycle stages as shown in Figure 4.23.

The lifecycle diagram contains details of the processes described in each of the five life cycle stages, together with the main outputs of each lifecycle stage. The problem management process is one of the five processes within the operational stage of the service lifecycle.

167

Figure 4.23 The ITIL lifecycle

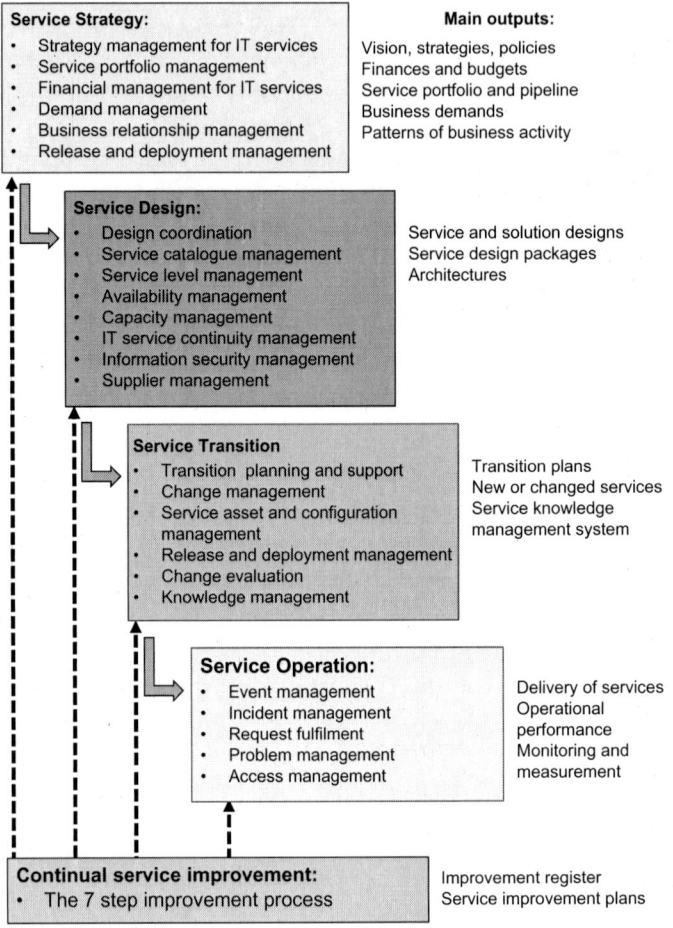

Service Strategy:
- Strategy management for IT services
- Service portfolio management
- Financial management for IT services
- Demand management
- Business relationship management
- Release and deployment management

Main outputs:
Vision, strategies, policies
Finances and budgets
Service portfolio and pipeline
Business demands
Patterns of business activity

Service Design:
- Design coordination
- Service catalogue management
- Service level management
- Availability management
- Capacity management
- IT service continuity management
- Information security management
- Supplier management

Service and solution designs
Service design packages
Architectures

Service Transition
- Transition planning and support
- Change management
- Service asset and configuration management
- Release and deployment management
- Change evaluation
- Knowledge management

Transition plans
New or changed services
Service knowledge
management system

Service Operation:
- Event management
- Incident management
- Request fulfilment
- Problem management
- Access management

Delivery of services
Operational
performance
Monitoring and
measurement

Continual service improvement:
- The 7 step improvement process

Improvement register
Service improvement plans

ITIL describes a problem management process based on managing a problem through its lifecycle. While there is an aspect of managing a problem through its lifecycle, in reality managing problems within a service provider environment is more complex and might involve many activities and techniques. These activities and techniques might often be used repetitively or in parallel in order to minimise their impact and to resolve the problem speedily (see page 77).

Figure 4.24 The ITIL problem management process flow

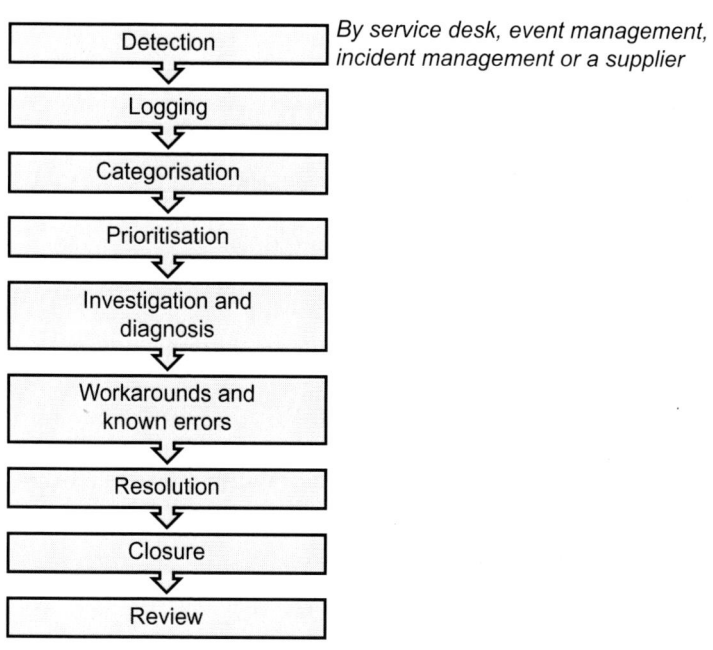

The following paragraphs contain a brief description of the key steps within the ITIL problem management process as shown in Figure 4.24.

Problem detection

There are two ways of detecting and identifying a problem:

- Reactively:
  - Identification of a situation where several incidents are occurring with similar symptoms and a problem record needs to be logged to allow the underlying cause to be investigated and resolved.
  - An incident with a major impact has occurred and a problem needs to be logged to allow the underlying cause to be investigated and resolved.
  - Analysis of an incident by the technical support team or a supplier or information from them

indicates that a problem exists within their area and needs to be resolved.

- Automated event detection (e.g. infrastructure, application monitoring tools) creates an incident that necessitates the creation of a problem record.
- Analysing user and customer feedback and complaints.

• Proactively:

- Analysis of incident records indicates that an underlying problem(s) exist and needs to be resolved.
- Trending of incident records and volumes indicate that an underlying problem(s) exists and needs to be resolved.
- Service improvement activities result in the need to raise a problem record to resolve a potential issue and improve the quality of a service.

Problem logging

All of the relevant details of the problem must be recorded so that a full description of the problem is recorded. This should include:

- problem description;
- user details;
- service details;
- component details;
- date and time the problem was initially logged;
- problem category;
- problem priority;
- relationships to associated incidents;
- details of associated diagnostic and additional information;
- details of any actions taken.

Problem categorisation

Problem records should be categorised in the same way as incidents, ideally using the same category codes. This supports:

- better matching and linking of incident and problem records;
- consistent management information and reporting across both incident and problem management activities.

Problem prioritisation

Problems should be prioritised in a similar way to incidents. The priority of a problem should be based on:

- the frequency and impact of related incidents;
- the availability and quality of any known errors and workarounds;
- the urgency of the problem;
- the severity of the problem, for example:
  - can the system be recovered; or
  - the cost of resolution;
  - the resources and skills needed to resolve the problem;
  - the time required to resolve the problem;
  - the scope or extent of the problem (e.g. the number of CIs affected).

Techniques such as pain value analysis (page 93), Pareto analysis (page 118) and others, as described elsewhere in this book, can be used to prioritise problems based on their business impact.

Problem investigation and diagnosis

The problem records should be reviewed and those with the highest priority should be investigated and diagnosed. Problem matching should be used on the known error database (KEDB) to determine if the problem has occurred previously. Any resolutions identified can then be applied to resolve the current problem. The configuration management system (CMS) should also be used to determine the impact of the problem and to identify and diagnose the underlying cause of the problem.

Sometimes the problem or failure can be recreated within development or testing environments. This simplifies the investigation, diagnosis and testing of resolutions without causing further disruption to users.

Techniques such as Kepner–Tregoe, A3 problem solving, Ishikawa, RCA and others, as described earlier, can be used to investigate, analyse and diagnose problems.

Identifying and implementing workarounds

It might be possible to identify and implement a workaround to reduce the impact of some problems (see page 78). When a workaround is found it is important that the problem record is kept open and the problem record is updated to refer to the workaround.

In some case multiple workarounds might be identified and implemented as the diagnosis of the problem progresses. Each workaround will hopefully reduce the business impact of the problem and therefore the priority of the problem should be reviewed and revised after each workaround has been implemented.

Raising known error records

A known error is a problem with a documented root cause and workaround. Therefore a known error record, contained within the KEDB, should refer to the problem it relates to, the root cause and the workaround. If further incidents and problems occur, then the workaround can be identified and the service can be quickly restored. Known error records should be created as soon as it becomes useful to do so (see page 78).

Problem resolution

Once a solution to the underlying root cause of the problem has been identified, it should be tested and applied. If changes in functionality to CIs are required, then a request for change (RFC) should be raised and authorised before the resolution is implemented. If an urgent resolution is required for business reasons, then an emergency RFC should be raised.

It might not be cost-effective to resolve the problem, for instance where the cost of doing so is prohibitive. In this case the problem record should remain open and the known error record and workaround should be used to resolve the incidents(s) quickly.

Problem closure

Once the problem has been finally resolved and confirmed with any affected users, the problem record can be closed. At this time any related incidents should also be closed. The contents of the problem record and any related records should be reviewed for accuracy and updated if necessary.

Major problem review

Each organisation should have a description and set of criteria that define a major problem. Once a major problem has been resolved, a formal review, the major problem review (MPR), should be completed as part of the closure procedure.

More information on MPRs can be found on page 145. The output from these reviews provides a vital source of information to proactive problem management because it can often give valuable input to service reviews and the continual service improvement (CSI) register.

Finally, a cautionary note concludes this section – one of the main reasons for the failure of service management implementations or improvement projects is that organisations try and implement a problem management process based closely on the guidance contained within the ITIL books. This approach is generally doomed to failure. The key phrase to remember with ITIL is 'adopt and adapt'. An organisation needs to adapt the guidance to fit its own people, business, legal and regulatory requirements. This holds true in particular to the problem management process described in ITIL because it is a process with a single workflow as shown in Figure 4.24, whereas problem management in practice is much more than that (see page 60).

Managing problems and problem records through their lifecycle is an important problem management activity. However, there are also many other important activities to be performed by problem managers and focusing exclusively on the problem lifecycle has prevented many problem managers from delivering real benefit to the business, customers and users.

The other key point is that a problem management process should be established in small incremental steps, rather than in one 'big bang' implementation. These small steps should be based around the already existing incident and problem management practices within the organisation, building and expanding the good aspects and reducing and removing the not-so-good ones.

COBIT®

COBIT® is a framework for the governance and management for enterprise IT. It comprises a set of publications and documents providing extensive guidance on enablers for the governance and management of IT.

Like ITIL, the COBIT® 5 framework also contains a comprehensive set of information relating to a set of management processes and activities. COBIT® provides advice and guidance on the governance of IT. The overall process reference model for COBIT® is shown in Figure 4.25. This diagram is contained in the document, COBIT 5 – Enabling Processes.[12] The information relating to problem management activities is contained in

---

[12] ISACA® (2012) COBIT 5 – Enabling Processes. ISACA®

Figure 4.25 The COBIT® process reference model (Source: COBIT 5: Enabling Processes, Figure 10, page 24.)

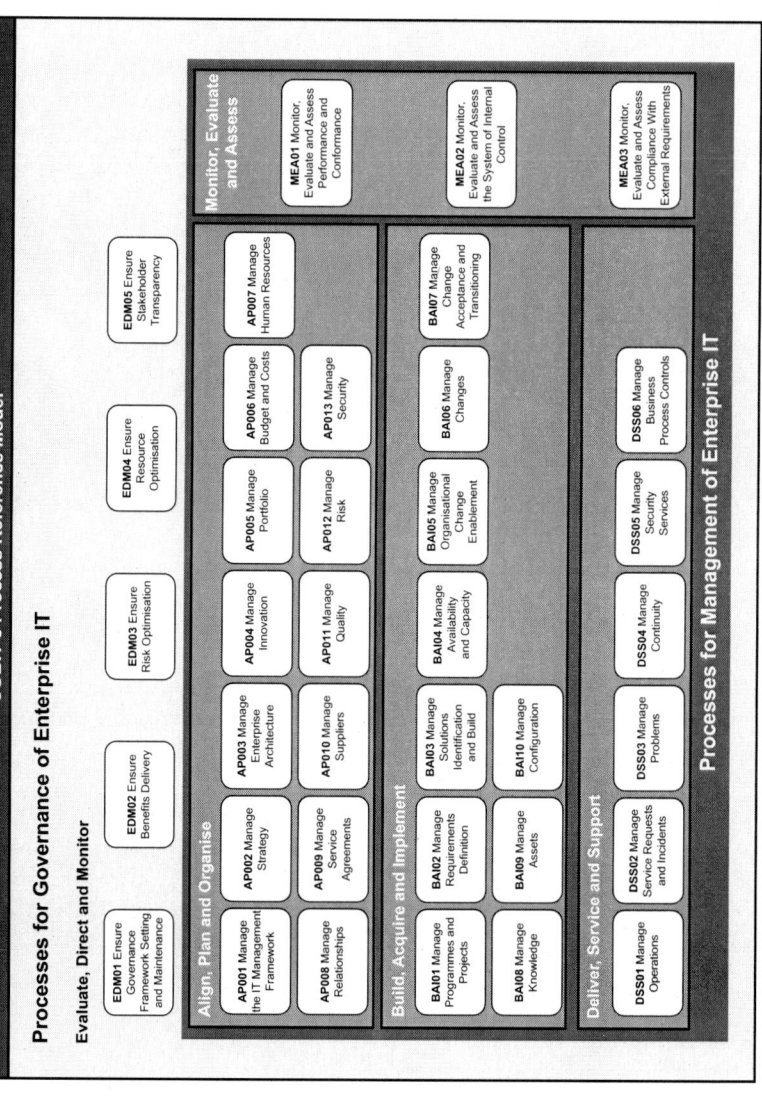

COBIT 5 Process Reference Model

Processes for Governance of Enterprise IT

Evaluate, Direct and Monitor

| EDM01 Ensure Governance Framework Setting and Maintenance | EDM02 Ensure Benefits Delivery | EDM03 Ensure Risk Optimisation | EDM04 Ensure Resource Optimisation | EDM05 Ensure Stakeholder Transparency |

Align, Plan and Organise

| AP001 Manage the IT Management Framework | AP002 Manage Strategy | AP003 Manage Enterprise Architecture | AP004 Manage Innovation | AP005 Manage Portfolio | AP006 Manage Budget and Costs | AP007 Manage Human Resources |
| AP008 Manage Relationships | AP009 Manage Service Agreements | AP010 Manage Suppliers | AP011 Manage Quality | AP012 Manage Risk | AP013 Manage Security | |

Monitor, Evaluate and Assess

| MEA01 Monitor, Evaluate and Assess Performance and Conformance |
| MEA02 Monitor, Evaluate and Assess the System of Internal Control |
| MEA03 Monitor, Evaluate and Assess Compliance With External Requirements |

Build, Acquire and Implement

| BAI01 Manage Programmes and Projects | BAI02 Manage Requirements Definition | BAI03 Manage Solutions Identification and Build | BAI04 Manage Availability and Capacity | BAI05 Manage Organisational Change Enablement | BAI06 Manage Changes | BAI07 Manage Change Acceptance and Transitioning |
| BAI08 Manage Knowledge | BAI09 Manage Assets | BAI10 Manage Configuration | | | | |

Deliver, Service and Support

| DSS01 Manage Operations | DSS02 Manage Service Requests and Incidents | DSS03 Manage Problems | DSS04 Manage Continuity | DSS05 Manage Security Services | DSS06 Manage Business Process Controls |

Processes for Management of Enterprise IT

the section on Deliver, Service and Support (DSS), under the Manage Problems process subsection (DSS03). Full information on the COBIT® 5 framework can be obtained from the ISACA® website at www.isaca.org.

The process for managing problems is described in COBIT® as one that identifies and classifies problems and their root causes. It also provides timely resolutions to prevent recurring incidents and recommendations for improvement. Its purpose is to improve service levels and availability, reduce costs and improve customer satisfaction.

A set of IT-related goals and metrics and process goals are also provided within the COBIT® documentation of the Manage Problems process. These are summarised in Tables 4.11 and 4.12.

Table 4.11 COBIT® – Manage problems (DSS03): IT-related goals and metrics (Source: COBIT 5: Enabling Processes, page 185.)

IT-related goal	Related metrics
Managing IT-related business risk	• Frequency of risk profile updates • Percentage of enterprise risk assessments including IT-related risks • Percentage of critical business processes and programmes including risk assessments • Number of major IT-related incidents, not identified in risk assessment

(Continued)

Table 4.11 (Continued)

IT-related goal	Related metrics
Aligning the delivery of services with business requirements	• Percentage of stakeholders satisfied with agreed levels of service • Percentage of users satisfied with IT service delivery • Number of business disruptions caused by service incidents
Optimising the use of IT assets, resources and capabilities	• Frequency of capability maturity and cost assessments • Level of business and IT executive satisfaction with resources and capabilities • Trend of assessment results
Providing reliable and accurate information for decision making	• Number of business process incidents caused by non-availability of information • Level of user satisfaction with accuracy and availability of information • Ratio and extent of erroneous business decisions where erroneous or unavailable information was a key factor

Table 4.12 COBIT® – Manage problems (DSS03): process goals and metrics

Process goal	Related metrics
Resolving problems so they do not recur	• Percentage of major incidents with related problems • Decrease in recurring incidents caused by unresolved problems • Number of problems with root cause resolution • Percentage of acceptable workarounds available for open problems • Percentage of problems associated with proactive problem activities

Further information is provided within COBIT® relating to supporting problem management practices. This information relates to the activities that constitute each of the five management practices:

- **Identify and classify problems (DSS03.01)** – Define and use procedures and criteria for managing problems, including the following activities:

  - Identify and record problems categorised and prioritised on business risk and service criticality.

  - Manage problems based on all relevant data, including information from change, configuration/asset and incident management.

  - Define appropriate support and resolver groups to assist problem management, based on defined categories (e.g. hardware, software, database).

- Define priority levels in consultation with the business basing levels on business impact and urgency ensuring problem activities are completed appropriately.

- Report problem status to the service desk so customers and management are informed appropriately.

- Maintain a single register of problems, report problems and establish audit trails, including problem status.

- **Investigate and diagnose problems (DSS03.02)** – Use resolver groups to assess and analyse root causes appropriately, with the following activities:

  - Identify and classify problems as a known error, where appropriate.

  - Associate problems/known errors with affected configuration items.

  - Monitor activities and produce reports on problem resolution progress and the status of the problem-handling process.

- **Raise known errors (DSS03.03)** – Identify and create known error records, acceptable workarounds and potential solutions of problems once the root cause has been established:

  - Progress and implement solutions to known errors based on business impact and cost benefit.

- **Resolve and close problems (DSS03.04)** – Identify and instigate resolutions of the root cause of problems, raising changes via change management. Ensure appropriate personnel are aware of all plans and actions for the prevention of future incidents.

  - Close problem records after confirmation of successful resolution of the known error or problem.

  - Ensure the service desk is aware of the schedule and consequences of known error and problem resolutions and inform users and customers.

- Regularly monitor the progress of problem changes and resolutions.

- Monitor the service impact of ongoing problems and known errors.

- Review and confirm the success of major problem resolutions.

- Make sure knowledge learnt from the problem review is recorded, communicated and made available.

- **Perform proactive problem management (DSS03.05)** – Gather and examine data to identify emerging trends and then create and analyse problem records:

  - Collect and analyse problem information and trends, particularly from incident and change records to identify and instigate potential corrective actions.

  - Ensure that known problems and planned changes are regularly discussed with other relevant areas.

  - Monitor and report on the total cost of problem management process activities.

  - Monitor and report on the progress of problem resolution against targets, ensuring escalation of problems and associated changes according to agreed criteria.

  - Optimise the use of resources and reduce workarounds: track problem trends.

  - Identify and instigate permanent resolutions of problem root causes raising appropriate changes.

COBIT® gives very good guidance on the goals that should be used in an organisation to achieve effective management of problems. It also contains very good advice on the metrics that should be used and the essential practices, inputs, outputs and activities that are needed to achieve the defined goals. More comprehensive problem management information is contained within the COBIT® 5 documentation.

TOOLS

This section considers some of the tools that are currently available to assist the problem manager with some of the activities and processes required within their area of responsibility. Some of the tools are self-help facilities for users of the services, enabling them to resolve issues for themselves without the need to contact the service desk. These facilities are very useful for access to request, incident and change records, but need to be used with care when providing access to problem records.

As mentioned before, it is important that processes and practices are selected and designed first before choosing the tool(s), even though the process might subsequently have to be 'tweaked' or adjusted to fit the requirements of the tool as a compromise. The alternative is often a lot of unnecessary time and resource spent in customising and tailoring the tool to meet the specific, additional requirements of the process.

The tools for specific areas of problem management are described in the following sections.

Managing problems through their lifecycle

There are many tools that provide the ability to manage problems through their lifecycle using problem records within a problem management system. These tools might be stand-alone problem tools or they might be fully integrated service management toolsets supporting many other service management processes. Many of the tools support the ITIL workflow and problem record lifecycle.

The majority of these tools recognise the need to differentiate between incident records and problem records and their separate needs, workflows and lifecycles. Some of them will support the definition of problem models and associated workflows. This means that teams and roles can be allocated to particular tasks to be performed within a timescale. If tasks are not completed within the agreed schedule, then the problem record can be escalated to a problem manager and remedial action can be instigated.

Managing known errors, workarounds and knowledge articles through their lifecycle

Many of the tools that manage problems through their lifecycle also provide the ability to manage known errors and workarounds. This capability is also part of the ITIL workflow within the problem record lifecycle and is included within the functionality of tools that implement the ITIL problem lifecycle. It provides important integration between problem management and service desk and incident management. This ability is supported by an underpinning known error database (KEDB). The more capable tools also provide the ability to link the records within the KEDB to problem records within the problem management system.

Some of these more comprehensive tools also offer an integrated service knowledge management system (SKMS), which allows knowledge articles to be stored. These records can contain any relevant information that can be used to assist with the resolution of incidents and problems, or just additional information that can be used to improve the incident management or problem management processes. The types of information that can be stored are many and varied, but can include:

- known errors and workarounds;
- diagnostic scripts;
- lessons learnt from major incident reviews;
- lessons learnt from major problem reviews;
- lessons learnt from project and programme reviews;
- support documentation.

The main challenge with all of these systems is that of information retrieval, and this aspect of the SKMS needs to be very carefully designed and implemented. There is no point in putting information into an SKMS if no one can find it. The more advanced tools in this area suggest closely related records and information as new records and information are being entered into the system. For example, if an incident is being entered into the system, the tool searches for other incident, problem and known error records for 'matches' or similar records. If any are found they are presented as a list of options to be selected or linked to the record being entered.

Analysing and reporting tools for problem types, volumes and trends

Many problem management tools provide comprehensive reporting facilities. Some of the most important areas of reporting for problem management include:

- outstanding open problems and the backlog of problems, overall totals and by priority;
- numbers and trends in major problems;
- trends in problems and problem areas;
- problems by service;
- problems by category, support area or technology area;
- problems by root cause.

More information on report types and reporting is contained on page 132.

Tools for linking problems to other entities

In order to understand the causes of problems and incidents and to analyse and prevent their recurrence, it is essential that problem records are linked to the CIs identified as the root cause. This is a very useful way of identifying key areas of 'pain' caused by incidents and problems and is one of the key advantages of an integrated service management toolset, although external links to other systems can also be useful. The main links of particular use to the management of problems are:

- incidents;
- changes;

- releases;
- requests;
- known errors and workarounds;
- services;
- the CMS and other CIs.

Problem analysis tools

There are also several tools that are of great help during the problem analysis stage of the lifecycle. Some of the key tools in this area are:

- creative problem solving (CPS) tools;
- Kepner–Tregoe tools;
- lean A3 tools.

Service portal

A service portal can greatly improve the quality and value of service delivered to the customers and users. A service portal with relevant information can provide users with access to information that enables them to answer their own queries and issues. When the service desk, incident management and problem management work closely together in a coherent manner, they can provide accurate and up-to-date information in their systems and the service desk tool and service knowledge management system (SKMS). If the customers and users can answer their own questions by accessing the information directly, there will be no need for them to refer to the service desk, as shown in Figure 4.26 (which is a development of Figure 2.2 on page 10).

The better the information and the accessibility of the information, the more likely the customers and users are to make use of the service portal and there will be less need for the service desk. This is the so-called 'shift left' initiative, where suitable and relevant information is shifted as far to the

Figure 4.26 Service portal

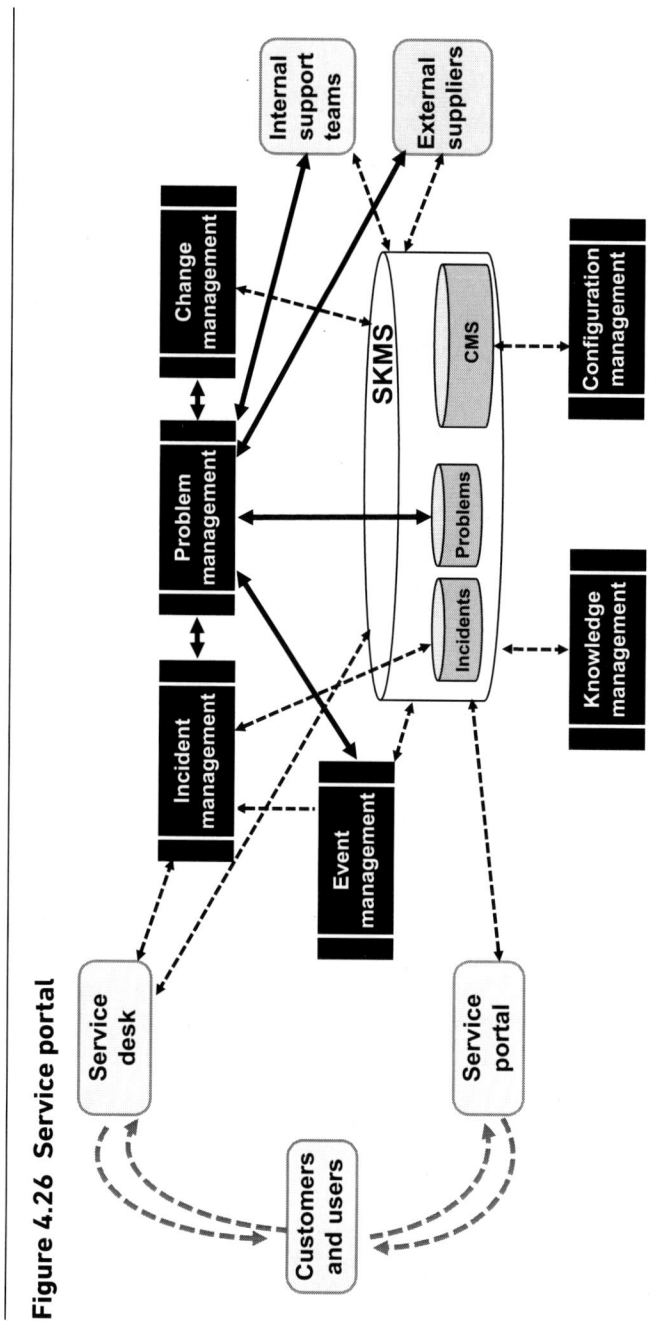

left of the diagram as is appropriate. This not only enables the service desk to provide an improved level of service, but it also provides greater openness and transparency to customers and users. Therefore the objective of all areas, not just incident and problem management, should be to improve the accuracy and value of the information provided by the service portal.

Other areas of problem functionality

There are many other problem tools available that can help with the management and resolution of problems. There are also many integrated service management tools that don't just provide problem management functionality, but also support capability in many other service management process areas. These integrated tools allow for automating interactions and interfaces between many of the areas described earlier in Chapter 3. They also support the linking of problem records to many other associated records, such as incidents, known errors, workarounds, changes, knowledge articles and CIs.

Other tools of value to problem management are statistical analysis tools, which provide the capability of analysing data and producing trends. These can be basic spreadsheet-type tools or purpose-built statistical processing software.

Reporting and presentation tools are helpful when the data has been analysed, helping to present the information simply and graphically to aid understanding and interpretation.

Another very important and valuable tool for problem managers is an action tracking tool, which allows agreed actions to be recorded, monitored, analysed and reported. Such a tool is invaluable in the management of actions produced from problem management activities, in particular those arising from PIR and MPR meetings. It helps to ensure that agreed actions are implemented on time or are automatically escalated if not. This is an essential aspect of a problem manager's role – automating the task of monitoring the progress of actions and removes the need for a lot of problem management manual effort and resource.

5   CAREER PROGRESSION AND RELATED ROLES

Problem management can provide a good career path for anybody with the right skills, knowledge and attributes. The last of these, attributes, is probably the most important.

A problem manager does not have to be a specialised technical person, and sometimes this can even prove a disadvantage as technical people often get entrenched or 'bogged down' in the technical detail of a problem, rather than focusing on the overall outcome required.

Problem managers can come from anywhere within the organisation, however problem management is often seen as a career path for personnel working on the service desk or working within the incident management process. They have the advantage of a good knowledge on the working of both the service desk and the incident management process, providing them with a good background knowledge and set of skills useful for working within problem management. They are also likely to have a good understanding of the business and a customer service focus, both of which are important when working within problem management.

The role of problem analyst is often seen as a career progression opportunity for a service desk analyst with the appropriate attributes. SFIA suggests that people working in service desk and incident management operate between levels 1 to 5 of the SFIA framework, and a service desk analyst, who would operate at level 3 or 4, could transfer and become a problem analyst, probably operating initially at level 3 or 4, but could then rise to a problem manager operating at level 5 of the framework.

From a problem manager, there are several further opportunities. If there is a preference to stay within the problem manager area, there could be opportunities for someone to take on additional responsibility and progress to the role of either problem management process owner or problem management process manager. These two roles are discussed earlier in Chapter 3.

Problem solving and decision making are key skills required of any manager. Working as a problem manager, a problem management process owner or a problem management process manager provides an ideal opportunity for someone to develop and master these areas. This then opens up many opportunities to move into other areas of management.

Some of the more common areas for problem managers, problem management process owners or problem management process managers to transfer to are:

- availability management;
- risk management;
- continual service improvement;
- IT service continuity.

These areas are particularly suited to people who have extensive experience of working in the proactive aspects of problem management.

6 CASE STUDIES

CASE STUDY 1

The IT service provider organisation of a financial services company had a service desk that provided support for operational services. Many of the applications it uses are either developed by the IT service provider organisation or customised by them.

They had a good incident management process, but no problem management activities. The organisation was experiencing increasing volumes of recorded incidents in total, but particularly in one area. Analysis of incidents didn't reveal anything because the categorisation of incidents was poor and the use of the incident categories was not good. All development and testing issues were recorded in a separate defects logging system and there was no differentiation between incidents and service requests.

The customers and users were complaining that IT did not address their key issues quickly enough and that many of their incidents would occur time and time again.

The organisation decided to start implementing problem management. They decided on the following problem activities in order to start making progress with problem management.

- Review and revise the incident categorisation system.

- Start recording service requests separately within the incident management system.

- Start recording problem records within the incident management system.

- Log defects identified during development and testing as problem records.

- Provide training in all areas on the use of incidents, service requests and problems, particularly for the service desk staff and the resolver groups.

They used the revised categorisation system for the categorisation of both incident and problem records. Once a new release had gone live, they linked incident or request occurrences to an existing problem record. If there wasn't a suitable problem record, they created a new one.

After a month, they produced reports on the analysis of problems and incidents using the new categorisation system. Some interesting discoveries were made:

- 80 per cent of incidents were service requests;

- over 80 per cent of service requests were for ten key reports;

- the total number of incident records in one area was 1,200.

They used this analysis and information to prioritise the order in which defects and requests were to be addressed and resolved. They then used the volumes of incidents and requests to justify to senior management the need for some development resources to be made available to address the key issues identified. The proposal was to develop a self-service portal for handling report requests.

Problem management then performed some basic requirements analysis for a solution and a business case. The proposed solution required ten days of development effort. This request was initially rejected by IT management because all development resources were tied up on key business development projects.

At this point, the analysis of the situation showed that the average service request took seven days to fulfil, of which 6.5 days was waiting time and 0.5 days was the time taken to actually fulfil the request. Therefore in one month for one key reporting area approximately 600 (1200 × 0.5) days of effort was spent producing reports. However, there was still no management backing because this was operational support effort and was very low priority for development resources.

Meanwhile users were still waiting for reports and external customers were experiencing delays in receiving information. The business users were still upset with the level of service with regards to the fulfilment of requests, especially for customer requested reports, so the operational support management discussed and explained the situation to business stakeholders. The business decided to defer one enhancement from the current planned release schedule to free up the development resource required.

The top ten reports were automated in a self-service portal, and user documentation and training was provided on how to use it. The use of the portal was good, resulting in a major reduction in service requests. Resolver groups carried on linking service requests to problem records, which were prioritised by business stakeholders. One additional report was added to the self-service portal each month. Within 12 months there were no new additional service requests for reports.

This activity led to a significant improvement in user and external customer satisfaction. Service desk staff numbers were reduced and operational support resources had more time to concentrate on project, release and deployment activities. This gave problem management the credibility, both within the business and IT, to start looking at further areas for improvement.

Operations still had had no real way of prioritising requests for improvement. The organisation was still very much business-driven and project-based.

The problem manager also assumed the role of CSI manager. A project was created for the improvement of support issues, with a requirement for dedicated development resource. A register of prioritised improvements was created and a proposal was created for a project addressing support issues and improvements. A request for a small, dedicated development resource was raised. The register and project were discussed with key business and IT stakeholders, and stakeholder commitment and approval obtained, based on past experience.

A 'service forum' was instigated by the problem manager, consisting of 'super users' from within the business. This forum was used to review and prioritise all support issues and improvements.

Training packs and 'crib sheets' were created on how to use the tool. Workshops and communication were organised for all support and development teams on training and 'upskilling' the support capability. Wherever possible teams would transfer knowledge and information from third-line support to second-line and from second-line support to first-line and the service desk.

It was now required that every incident record must be linked to a problem record, either a record that existed or a newly created 'candidate' for a problem record. This candidate record was sent to a support team lead who reviewed each candidate record and either accepted it, revised the details and assigned it to a development team or rejected it. Each of these actions required just a single mouse button click, so there was very little extra effort.

A monthly report of the outstanding problem backlog, showing volumes of linked incidents, was produced and distributed to the 'service forum'. The numbers of linked incidents was used as an indicator of the business impact/disruption or 'pain value'. The issues were discussed and prioritised by the 'service forum' and a list was formed for implementation.

A very simple problem management process was implemented within the tool. If the problem record status for a problem was 'awaiting assessment', then it would not be looked at by IT support or development until approved by the 'service forum'. Once approved, the problem record status was set to 'estimate to fix root cause'. The record was then referred back to the 'service forum' with this estimate. The forum would either approve it for resolution or defer it.

A change was then raised, linked to the problem record for each approved problem, and the status was set to 'developing fix' status. The change was scheduled for the next available release of the service. Once implemented the status was set to 'waiting PIR' and referred back to the relevant support team. The PIR was based on a business cycle, which was different for each service. If no incidents were raised before the business cycle had elapsed, then the problem and change records were closed as successful. If any incidents were raised during the business cycle then the change was marked as a 'failed' change and the root cause of the problem was re-investigated.

Once this improvement project had been running for six months a benefits realisation review was completed with the business stakeholders and the 'service forum'. The findings were as follows:

- Business benefits:
  - Business stakeholders were getting 10–20 per cent more changes and development projects in each release, from just 90 per cent of the resource they used to have.
  - There was increased focus and progress with strategic projects.
  - Less time was wasted on raising and chasing calls, incidents and requests.
- IT benefits:

  - Increased use of the self-service portal with a corresponding decrease in the number of service desk calls. Also incident volumes dropped considerably.

- Reduction of service desk staff.

- Increased capability and productivity of first-, and second-line support from 'upskilling' activities.

- Less disruption and demand for second- and third-line support, allowing them to focus more on strategic development and project activity.

CASE STUDY 2

The IT services for a worldwide publishing company were provided by an internal IT service provider organisation. The IT organisation consisted of some 300 personnel with the structure shown in Figure 6.1.

Figure 6.1 Case study 2 – Organisational structure and responsibilities (Source: COBIT 5: Enabling Processes, page 185.)

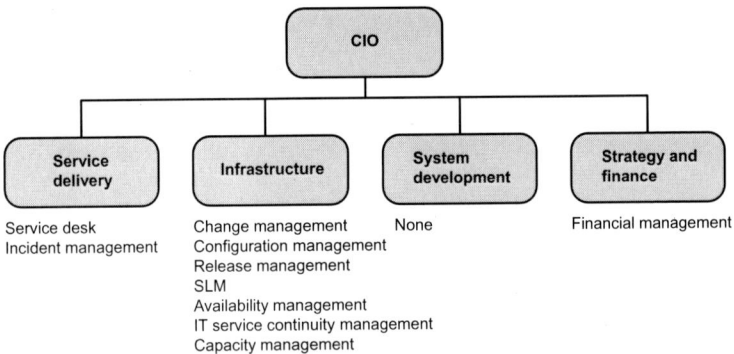

The organisation had not spent much time on the implementation of any of the service management processes. A new CIO was appointed and decided that he wanted to be more aligned with the needs of the business and customers and decided to embark upon a service improvement plan (SIP). He decided to study for the ITIL Manager's certificate in service management and passed the exams. He then encouraged many of his staff to attend ITIL training courses.

The starting point for the SIP would be the completion of a maturity assessment of the service management processes by an external organisation. The initial results of this assessment are shown in Figure 6.2.

Figure 6.2 Case study 2 – Initial maturity assessment

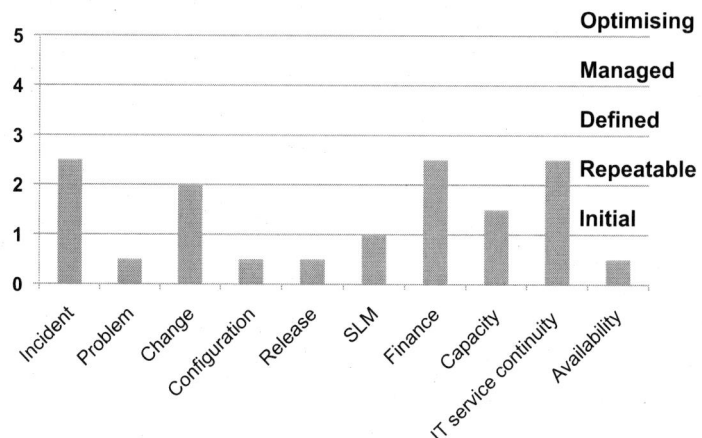

The general issues identified by this assessment were:

- a lack of involvement from development staff in operational aspects of service and applications;
- a task-oriented culture relying on people's knowledge and skills, rather than documented procedures;
- local processes and procedures used within teams, sections and functions rather than centralised and common ones throughout the department;
- some areas of IT not following any processes;
- no integration or linking between processes;
- a technology focus with little emphasis on services.

The review showed that both the processes and the organisation were relatively immature.

As a result of this assessment, the CIO decided that a SIP covering all ten processes should be initiated. The objective of the SIP was to raise the maturity of all service management processes to 'defined' (level 3), as illustrated in the maturity assessment diagram (Figure 6.2).

The responsibility for the improvement of the service management functions and processes was allocated between some of the IT sections, with the section manager being accountable for their improvement. The allocated responsibilities are illustrated in the organisational diagram (Figure 6.1). One of the team leaders within the infrastructure section was made responsible for the improvement of capacity, problem and configuration management. He had previously been responsible for capacity management of the mainframes.

An external service management specialist was engaged to deliver training and provide guidance and assistance for each process owner. Small virtual teams were established for each process and foundation training was provided for each person involved in service management activities. Also a 'brainstorming' workshop was conducted for each process team to identify the activities and timescales needed to progress each of the processes. The infrastructure manager, who was the overall project manager, collected all of these together into an overall project plan. The progress of this plan was reviewed on a regular basis, which was reported monthly to the CIO. The milestones and objectives became part of the overall IT objectives. A process template document was produced so that each process definition was in the same format. A central shared area was established for all of the plans and documents, with appropriate document controls.

Each process owner was asked to ensure that their process documentation contained:

- an overall description, scope, purpose, objectives and policy;
- a set of roles and responsibilities;
- a set of process deliverables;

- a set of interfaces to other processes;
- a process definition;
- a set of activities, within an overall process flow.

They were also encouraged to start thinking about process metrics.

Once the documents had been produced each process owner then had to provide appropriate documentation and training on the process for all of the people who would be involved in using the process. Wherever possible the documentation would be contained within the service management tool. Once the documentation and training had been completed the process was implemented. The process owner was then responsible for the operation and management of the process.

The problem process defined at this point was very much based on ITIL version 2 and was based around the activities of:

- **Incident control** – Assisting incident management wherever required and ensuring that appropriate and consistent categorisation was used by both incident and problem management.

- **Problem control** – Managing problems through their lifecycle:
  - Identification and registration.
  - Classification (categorisation and impact).
  - Investigation and diagnosis.
  - Resolution and closure.

- **Error control** – Raising known errors and identifying, removing or replacing weak or failing components.

- **Management information** – Defining metrics and producing reports.

Once the project had been completed another maturity assessment review was completed with the results shown in Figure 6.3.

Figure 6.3 Case study 2 – Second maturity assessment

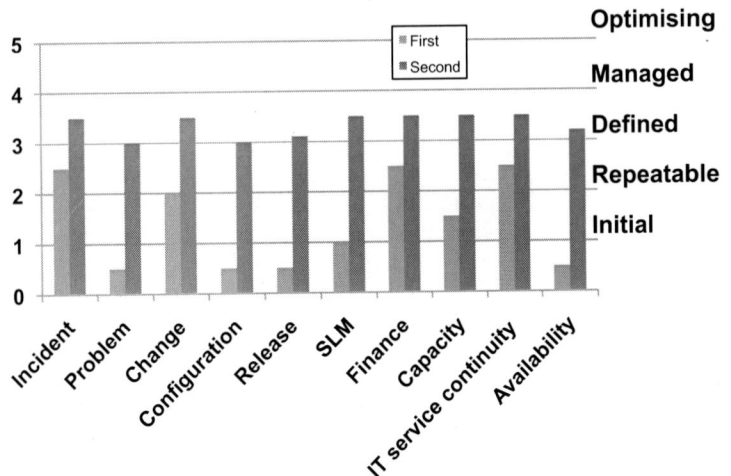

From this it can be seen that all of the processes approached or attained level 3 (defined). The 'problem' and 'configuration' processes did not reach level 3, principally due to:

- owning and managing two processes was too much for one person;

- the original incident management data was poor and was of little value to problem management – the improved service desk and incident management system had only been implemented within the last month, giving 'problem' little opportunity to progress.

- the process owner had concentrated more on capacity management, which was his main interest rather than 'configuration' and 'problem'.

At least problem management had achieved the level required to meet the objective of the CIO. However, the maturity assessment review revealed other areas that needed attention:

- There were very few process measurements in place.

- There was very little reporting from any of the processes.

- The processes were very bureaucratic and over complex in some areas, having been based on theory rather than the needs of the business and IT.

- Ten process silos had been implemented: there was very little integration between any of the processes.

- There was some conflict between process owners.

- There was little use of automation.

- There was little involvement of systems development within the service management activities.

The CIO first recognised and celebrated the success. He then reviewed the assessment report and, based on its content, made the following decisions and recommendations:

- Each process owner should only own one process.

- There must be greater involvement of systems development in the service management.

- Phase 2 of the SIP would be started.

- The emphasis of phase 2 would be in four areas:
  - The processes should be reviewed and wherever possible unnecessary activities should be removed.
  - Improved measurement and reporting.
  - Greater use of automation.
  - Greater integration between the processes.

Phase 2 of the SIP was initiated with a workshop involving all process owners, including the newly appointed process owners. Each process owner was again tasked with producing a process improvement plan. Specific workshops were again run for each individual process to 'brainstorm' ideas and plans for the next stage of process improvement. Another workshop was then run by the infrastructure manager who collated all of the process plans into an overall SIP. Again she was responsible for the management of the overall SIP and for providing the CIO with monthly updates.

The service desk manager moved from the service desk and was made the problem manager, and became the new problem management process owner. Significant progress was made because the new process manager had more time to devote to the problem process. Also, the service desk manager knew the incident management system well and could analyse the data. Problem measurements and metrics were put in place and reports were produced. However, there were still some issues with the process:

- Too many problem records were being created.

- Problem management became known as the 'problem police' and were always hassling and chasing resolver groups for progress, rather than adding any value.

- A considerable backlog of unresolved problems developed. It was difficult to focus on the 'real problems'.

- There was little focus on developing workarounds and known errors.

- There was a lack of knowledge on the service desk of problem information and activities.

- There was still a lack of involvement of system development staff in the problem management process.

So the process plan for 'problem' needed to be revised to address these issues. Another workshop with representatives from all resolver groups was conducted to discuss the issues and to review and revise the problem plan. As a result of the workshop the following actions and activities were agreed:

- The criteria for creating a problem record were revised so that fewer problem records were created.

- A short, concentrated exercise involving all resolver groups was initiated to reduce the problem backlog from over 500 outstanding problem records to under 100.

- A very practical workshop was conducted with all resolver groups focusing on the need and the importance of developing workarounds and known errors.

- Time was spent automating the process more. This, together with all of the other actions, greatly reduced the need for progress chasing resolver groups.

- Problem management started to get more involved with change management, by attending the change advisory board (CAB) and working together on reducing the number of failed changes.

- Problem workshops were held for service desk staff and system development staff:

  - The service desk workshop focused on the purpose of problem management and the value of matching incidents and linking incidents to problem records and known errors.

  - The system development workshop focused again on the purpose of problem management and how system development staff could assist the problem process. This principally concentrated on the issues and defects detected during development and testing, emphasising the need to make these known and available to problem management when new releases were handed over.

The revised plans were agreed with the overall project manager and were then shared with other process owners. All of the plans were completed and another maturity assessment was instigated, which produced the results shown in Figure 6.4.

All of the processes had reached a maturity level of approaching 3.5 or above. Problem management had reached a maturity level of 4 and was now being recognised as delivering value

Figure 6.4 Case study 2 – Third maturity assessment

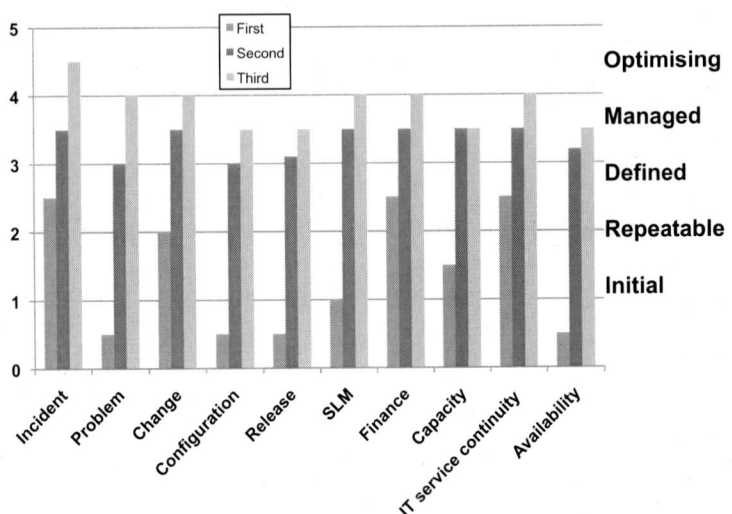

within both IT and the rest of the organisation. It was also starting to develop a proactive capability with good incident analysis and trending and, by working closely with availability management, on the reduction of service unavailability.

The CIO again recognised and celebrated the value and benefit that the service management programme and projects had delivered and realised it was time to consolidate these activities into business as usual. The quality team within the 'finance' section were asked to run the CSI process. The problem manager was made the liaison point with the quality team and asked to develop an even greater proactive problem management capability.

APPENDICES

A1 A3 PROBLEM-SOLVING REPORT TEMPLATE

Figure A1.1 A3 problem-solving report template

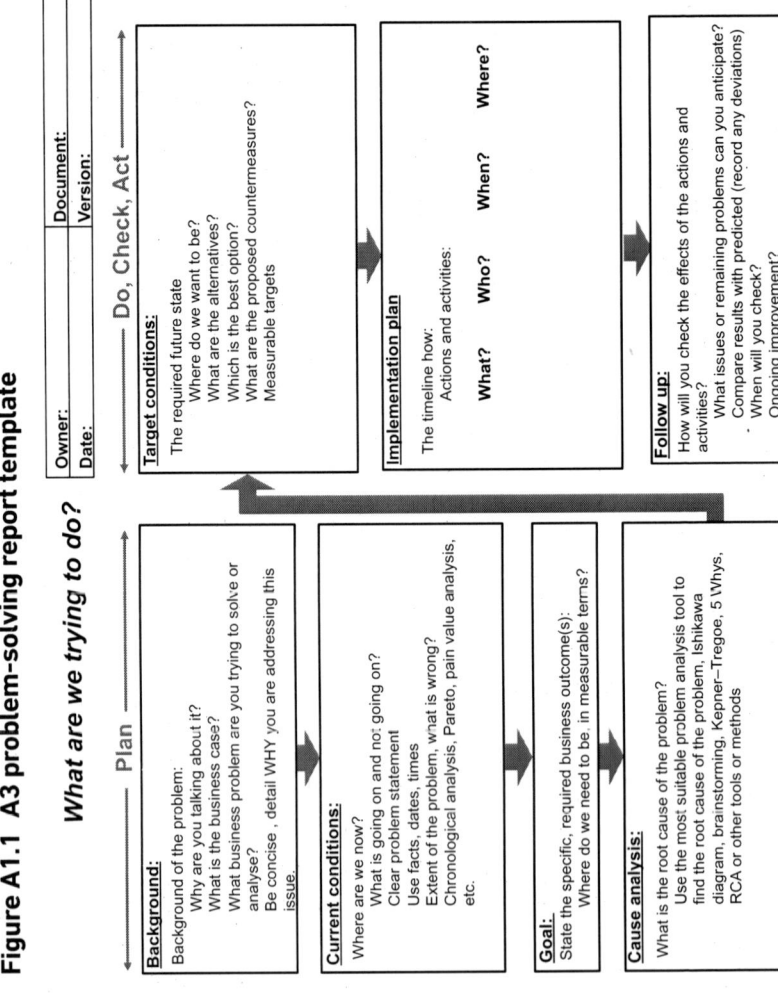

What are we trying to do?

Owner:	Document:
Date:	Version:

— Plan — ——— Do, Check, Act ———

Target conditions:

The required future state
- Where do we want to be?
- What are the alternatives?
- Which is the best option?
- What are the proposed countermeasures?
- Measurable targets

Implementation plan

The timeline how:
Actions and activities:

What? Who? When? Where?

Follow up:

How will you check the effects of the actions and activities?
- What issues or remaining problems can you anticipate?
- Compare results with predicted (record any deviations)
- When will you check?
- Ongoing improvement?

Background:

Background of the problem:
- Why are you talking about it?
- What is the business case?
- What business problem are you trying to solve or analyse?
- Be concise , detail WHY you are addressing this issue.

Current conditions:

Where are we now?
- What is going on and not going on?
- Clear problem statement
- Use facts, dates, times
- Extent of the problem, what is wrong?
- Chronological analysis, Pareto, pain value analysis, etc.

Goal:

State the specific, required business outcome(s):
- Where do we need to be, in measurable terms?

Cause analysis:

What is the root cause of the problem?
- Use the most suitable problem analysis tool to find the root cause of the problem, Ishikawa diagram, brainstorming, Kepner–Tregoe, 5 Whys, RCA or other tools or methods

A2   RISK ASSESSMENT AND MANAGEMENT TABLE

Table A2.1 Operational risk assessment example spreadsheet

Risk No	Owner	Risk description and impact	Probability	Impact	Risk rating	Probability	Impact	Risk rating	Status	Next review date	Mitigation (actions to reduce risk)	Contingency (action/cost should it occur)
1	AB	Failure of building A switch	2	2	4	2	2	4	Open	Next meeting		
2	BC	Failure of building B switch	2	1	2	2	1	2	Open	Next meeting		
3	CD	Failure of building C switch	2	4	8	2	2	4	Mitigated	Next year	Implement a second switch in building B	
4	DE	Failure of building D switch	2	1	2	2	1	2	Open	Next meeting		

(Continued)

Table A2.1 (Continued)

Risk No	Owner	Risk description and impact	Proba-bility	Impact	Risk rating	Proba-bility	Impact	Risk rating	Status	Next review date	Mitigation (actions to reduce risk)	Contingency (action/cost should it occur)
5	EF	Failure of building E switch	2	2	4	2	2	4	Open	Next meeting		
6	DC	Power failure or unavailability of data centre building (e.g. fire)	2	5	10	2	5	10	Planned	Next meeting	Install a generator on the data centre building planned	
7	LB	Load balancer failure	2	5	10	1	0	0	Closed	Next year	Install second load balancer	

(Continued)

Table A2.1 (Continued)

Risk No	Owner	Risk description and impact	Proba-bility	Impact	Risk rating	Proba-bility	Impact	Risk rating	Status	Next review date	Mitigation (actions to reduce risk)	Contingency (action/cost should it occur)
8	DB	Database server failure	2	5	10	2	4	8	Partially miti-gated	Next year	Continuously monitor the database server and automate its recovery	
9												
10			Original risk KPI:	50			Current risk KPI:	34				

A3 MAJOR PROBLEM REVIEW TEMPLATE

Table A3.1 Major problem review template

Major problem review (MPR)			
MPR date:		Next MPR date (if applicable):	

Problem / incident references:	
Problem references:	Incident references:
Problem status:	

Problem description – Management summary:		
Attendees:		
Problem manager:		
Lessons learnt:		
Incident details:		
Restoration actions		
Initial problem severity:	Final problem severity:	

Timeline (GMT) – Key dates and times should be completed below	
Detection:	
Actual start date/time:	

(Continued)

Table A3.1 (Continued)

First event/alarm date/time:	
First call date/time:	
Incident open time/date:	
Problem open date/time:	
Escalation:	
First resolver owner *(start of escalation)*:	
Final resolver owner *(final escalation)*:	
Severity 1 escalation *(if initial escalation not S1)*:	
Actions taken:	
Diagnosis date/time *(start of restoration)*:	
Restoration date/time *(service restored)*:	
Recovery end date/time *(service recovered)*:	
Communication:	
User customer communication *(date/time)*:	
Management communication *(date/time)*:	

Customer impact / Voice of the customer (VOC):
Total service desk call count: 0 – number customers impacted:

Root cause analysis:			
Trigger:			
Root cause:			
Workaround / Known error:			
Failure avoidance:			
Recovery questions	Yes	No	Comments
1 Was the incident releated to a change request?			
2 Was the incident releated to a known error?			

(Continued)

Table A3.1 (Continued)

Issue identification:	
Who first identified the issue?	
How was the issue first identified?	

Action items / opportunities for improvements:			
Item / Comments (*delete as applicable*)	Owner	Due date:	Status:
1 Action:			
2 Outcome:			

INDEX